THE VIETNAM WAR TRIVIA BOOK

Fascinating Facts and Interesting Vietnam War Stories

Trivia War Books Vol. 2

BY
BILL O'NEILL
DWAYNE WALKER

DON'T FORGET YOUR
FREE BOOKS

CONTENTS

INTRODUCTION

The Vietnam War. If you're living in the United States, you've heard of it… and if you don't live in the United States, you've heard of it too, although maybe in a slightly different context. It might be the most famous war in America that doesn't have "World" in the name. From the dozens of movies that use it as a backdrop, to the iconic art created by the anti-war movement, its influence on our culture today is enormous.

The Vietnam War lasted for twenty years, from 1955 to 1975—the longest war that the United States ever fought in. But it started even before that, with fighting between Vietnam and France—their old colonial overlords. Over time, it spilled into the famous America-versus-Vietnam crisis that most people in the west are familiar with now.

Hundreds of thousands of people died, both American and Vietnamese, civilians and soldiers. They died in horrible ways too, and their deaths were captured on camera and immortalized for all the

1

world to see. People were outraged. It was so devastating that just calling something "Vietnam" is more or less the same as calling it a complete disaster.

But was it really that simple? Why did the fighting turn out so badly?

Let me ask you, what do you *know* about the Vietnam War? Why was it being fought, and who fought it? Were there good guys and bad guys, or was it such a complicated mess that no one came out looking good at all? Who were the Viet Cong, the Viet Minh, and all the other groups that you hear about in books and movies?

By reading this book, you can get the answers to those questions—and many more that you didn't even know you had. The Vietnam War was complicated and confusing, but this book will guide you through its messy origins and teach you about why it unfolded the way it did. In short bite-sized pieces, you'll learn about the Cold War, communism, and capitalism. You'll learn why the United States was so scared of the spread of communism and why North Vietnam thought it looked like a pretty nice system. Then, we'll take you through the political fights and negotiations that led to the States being on the ground in Vietnam, even though there are dozens of quotes from leaders saying that was exactly what they *didn't* want to do.

From there, we're going to get in on the ground and really see what it was like to fight in the Vietnam War. You'll meet key players like Hồ Chí Minh and Lyndon B. Johnson, who appear in all the history books. But you'll also get acquainted with colorful characters like Peter Lemon and Roy Benavidez. You'll learn about the bizarre tactics that the armies used against each other like the Ace of Spades and Operation Wandering Soul. You'll meet the subjects of some of the famous photographs you may have seen, like the "napalm girl," "burning monk," and even "flower power"—pictures that are used by history teachers and documentaries every day, but that no one ever takes the time to really explain the background to.

We'll also go back to the States and meet the people protesting the war, from 82-year-old pacifist hero Alice Herz to poetic icon Allen Ginsberg. Sometimes the protests were dead serious, like the three people who set themselves on fire in America. Sometimes they were a little silly, like the protesters who put flowers inside police guns during their protests.

These are fun facts, but the Vietnam War wasn't fun. No matter how you look at it, it was a tragedy that shook people's faith in their own governments and even the ultimate goodness of the world. Even now, in 2017, we're still living in the fallout. Every time someone says they're suspicious of what the government might not be telling them about foreign affairs, they're being affected by the dissatisfaction that grew up in Vietnam. Every time Donald Trump says something outrageous to a foreign diplomat, he's adopting Richard Nixon's Vietnam War tactics. Every time you listen to the Beatles, you're listening to Vietnam War protestors.

By learning about the Vietnam War, you're also learning about the world today. With six easy chapters and hundreds of quick facts and intriguing details, reading this book will prepare you to see the world in a whole new light. No matter whether you're a student preparing for your next exam or just want to understand modern politics better, this is the book for you.

Each chapter is divided up into fifteen quick stories that will explain the complicated situations of the war in bite-sized pieces. They will also share the most interesting, important, or downright strange events of the Vietnam War, both in Vietnam and at home in America. They'll intrigue and entertain but also teach you cold hard facts that you can pull out at a dinner party or in history class. The stories are so short that you won't want to stop reading!

Each chapter also comes with twenty quick, surprising facts to wow your friends and five challenging trivia questions to test what you've learned that chapter.

Get ready to find out…

Who was important enough to be called Vietnam's George Washington?

Why did the United States get involved in Vietnam when it was such an unpopular choice?

Why is the Vietnam War called part of the Cold War… and just what *was* the Cold War?

What does Harris Tweed have to do with the draft?

And much, much more!

CHAPTER ONE

SETTING THE STAGE

The year? 1945. World War Two had ended, and the western world was celebrating the defeat of Adolf Hitler, history's most monstrous dictator! True, it ended with a sinister bomb, a so-called "weapon of mass destruction," which is now driving a wedge between two of the most important players in World War Two. And there's a little tension over in East Asia. The nation of "Indochina" is starting to rebel against the French leaders who have been in power for almost a century. A great rift is forming between countries that adhere to the communist political system and countries that support capitalism and democratic government. Tensions are running high… and not a single shot has been fired yet.

Communism and Capitalism

The core conflict that caused the Cold War and, eventually, became a key part of the Vietnam war was the fight between the United States and the

Soviet Union and their two different ideas about how the economy should work. The United States believed in the *capitalist* system—that people should be allowed to give their money to whomever they wanted, and that the people providing what they wanted should be able to take that money. On the other hand, the Soviet Union (also known as the *USSR*) believed in the *communist* or *socialist* system—that the government should control what work people were doing and what money they were getting for it, so that no one could be forced to work harder for fewer rewards than anyone else.

Both the US/capitalist side and the USSR/communist side of the war strongly believed that their type of economy was not only better for their people, but morally right. The USSR believed that capitalism exploited the poor and weak, forcing them to work themselves to death or in terrible conditions that they could not escape from. On the other hand, the US believed that communism put too much power in the hands of the government, who could then destroy the lives of everyone they disagreed with by taking away their money.

The problem was that both sides were right that both capitalism and communism had genuine problems. This made it very difficult for either side to come to a compromise or agreement, because they thought that if they allowed the other side any leeway at all, the bad aspects of capitalism or communism would immediately become problematic.

The Bomb

The Cold War is the name given to the series of tensions, espionage endeavors, and proxy-wars that took place between the Soviet Union and the United States over whether communism or capitalism should become the dominant type of economy all over the world. The Cold War lasted from the end of World War Two in 1945 to the collapse of the Soviet Union in 1991. This series of fights took place over almost fifty years and was a period of extreme anxiety for everyone involved.

Any disagreement that is based as strongly on morality as the one between communists and capitalists could be extremely dangerous and likely to cause damage. However, in the Cold War, there was an even bigger problem that people had to worry about: atomic weapons.

In 1945, at the very end of World War Two, the United States won the war by using two enormous atom bombs to destroy two major cities in Japan, one of their enemies in the war. These atom bombs were infinitely more powerful than the explosives that had been used in the past, even a few years before. People were shocked at the amount of power that a single weapon could have and, people started getting concerned that the United States knew how to make them. They feared that if a single country had control over such a devastating weapon, that country could effectively become the dictator over the entire world.

So, it wasn't long before the Soviet Union announced that they had also developed the technology for atomic weapons. Now, two countries—opposed to each other in almost every way—had technology that could wipe out entire cities in the blink of an eye. Surprisingly, this did not make people feel much more secure than they had felt when just the United States had the technology to make atomic bombs. Instead, they started to worry that if either country did anything the other country didn't like, they would fire off atomic bombs at each other, and the whole world could be destroyed in the crossfire. This problem—that both countries had world-ending technology that they could deploy at any moment—became known as "mutually assured destruction" or "MAD" for short.

What was the Cold War? Part 1: Competition and the Space Race

Neither the United States nor the Soviet Union really wanted to end the world if they could avoid it, so of course they were reluctant to start firing atomic weapons. But, at the same time, both countries wanted to keep the other country "in check." This led to a large number of tensions between the countries, especially when it came to competitions in developing technology,

Not all of the competitions between the United States and the Soviet Union were deadly. Probably the most constructive competition between the two nations was the Space Race. This was the struggle between the United States and the Soviet Union to "take control" of outer space by developing space travel technologies that had previously only been possible in science fiction. This was a competition that the USSR started when they fired *Sputnik 1* in 1955. *Sputnik 1* was the world's first human-made satellite. The Soviet Union fired it into space and from the ground people could see it orbiting the Earth.

Sputnik 1 didn't really do much of anything, except send out some radio waves that gave Soviet scientists some information about the ionosphere (the upper atmosphere in which it was orbiting). It was what the satellite represented that sent the Americans into a panic. If the Soviets could send a man-made satellite into space and make it orbit the earth so that it moved easily over the United States, what would happen if they attached a bomb onto a satellite and somehow rigged it to drop the bomb right over the States? The US had to prove that the Soviets couldn't have control over space. This led to both the United States and the Soviet Union rushing to create technology that could explore outer space. The Soviet Union had put the first satellite into space, and also sent the first human into space in 1961. In 1969, the United States put the first man on the moon with the Apollo 11 mission, which essentially pegged them as the winners of the Space Race.

What was the Cold War? Part 2: The Arms Race

The Space Race was not the only technological race between the United States and the Soviet Union during the Cold War period, and it was by far the most benign. While, in theory, space technology *could* be used as a weapon of war, ultimately putting a man in space or on the moon was more of a symbolic move than a military one. The same could not be said for the race between the United States and the Soviet Union to develop the greatest stockpiles of nuclear weapons. This struggle was known as the Nuclear Arms Race.

Immediately after World War Two, the United States was the only country that knew how to make nuclear weapons. However, the Soviet Union were working on their own versions, and they proved in 1949 that they had the technology to create nuclear weapons exactly like the ones the United States had made.

In 1952, the United States developed a hydrogen bomb that could kill all life for 100 miles. In 1953, the

Soviet Union created a bomb with a slightly smaller range, but that was small enough that it could be dropped out of an airplane. In 1954, the States detonated a bomb so big that people 300 miles away died of radiation poisoning, each country creating bigger, more convenient, and more powerful nuclear weapons to try to compete with the other country.

In the 1950s, a new type of missile was created—the intercontinental ballistic missile. These were based on German designs from World War Two and would have made it possible for the United States and the Soviet Union to send nuclear weapons over each other's countries without even having to fly an airplane.

Both sides – the United States and the Soviet Union – knew that the other side had enough nuclear weapons that, if attacked, they would be able to decimate the other country. This led to an unstable understanding of peace—both countries ready to attack in a moment's notice, but both not wanting to make the first move out of fear for themselves.

What was the Cold War? Part 3: Proxy Wars

So, both the United States and the Soviet Union really wanted to fight each other, but both were afraid of making a direct attack because they knew they would suffer a nuclear attack in return.

This led to the practice of fighting "proxy wars"—

wars fought between two countries that *weren't* the United States or the Soviet Union, but where the United States backed one side and the Soviet Union backed the other side.

Ultimately, this was how both the United States and the Soviet Union (and the various other countries that sided with either of them during the Cold War) viewed the war in Vietnam. It was a power play between capitalist and communist forces, and its main purpose was a show of dominance to prove what one side could do in battle without actually attacking a country that had nuclear weapons.

This was a huge part of the Vietnam War's origin, and it is how it is generally viewed by people who are not experts on the subject. However, the war was not necessarily viewed as having anything to do with communism or capitalism when it started out. Instead of being caused by the Cold War, it was caused by a long series of problems with colonial government in Vietnam and a fight over whether to unify it into one country or separate it into two.

France in Vietnam

Starting in the 1850s, Vietnam was under colonial control by France. The whole area was known in Europe as *French Indochina*—a name that was made up one hundred percent by Europeans and had absolutely nothing to do with the actual culture of

Vietnam, which was not French, Indian, or Chinese. What it was, was one of France's most significant colonial properties after they lost control of their holdings in North America. The area was rich in natural resources and was also nearby to important trading countries like China, which meant that it was in a very good strategic position from the French point of view.

Starting at the very beginning of French colonization, way back in the 1850s and '60s, there was resistance to French rule in the Vietnam area. Vietnamese people resented the way they were treated by what they felt was an oppressive foreign government. Many people lived in grinding poverty, especially in rural areas. There were many attempts at revolution, but none of the uprisings were very successful.

Everything changed in 1940. That was when France was invaded by Nazi Germany, and it was put under German control. This meant that France's Asian properties (all of which were collectively known as Indochina) were also under the control of the Nazis. At the same time, Japan (also a Nazi ally) invaded the area. The two governments collaborated, and the French allowed most of the power over the area to be held by the Japanese, not consulting the native inhabitants about the situation, of course.

This did not sit well with the native Vietnamese. They were outraged that France, the country that was professing to have ultimate and unshakable power over them, had handed over control of the country to Japan (their historical rival!) without even so much as putting up a fight. While independence movements in Vietnam had not had much success before this, the outrage caused by this transfer of power spurred on a new kind of push for independence.

Hồ Chí Minh and the Việt Minh

Việt Minh, or the League for the Independence of Vietnam, was founded by a popular political leader named Hồ Chí Minh.

Hồ Chí Minh had been born in a small Vietnamese village in 1890, but as a child, he quickly demonstrated that he was extremely intelligent and quick to learn. He studied Vietnamese writing, Chinese Writing, and theology. When he was a young man, he traveled the world by ship, including going to the United States. While he was travelling, he had encounters that shaped his view of the world and especially his politics. He saw the way that, all over the world, people were oppressed and mistreated by powerful and greedy leaders. He dreamed of developing a better future for his own underprivileged country.

Hồ Chí Minh was a socialist—a slightly less extreme form of communism. He believed that the government had a responsibility to help people who were being oppressed and downtrodden, and he strongly believed that the French government was never going to do that. That was why he became the leader of the Việt Minh movement for Vietnamese independence.

He had been a nationalist leader for Vietnam before and had tried in the 1930s to get some traction for an independence party without very much success. For decades, he petitioned the French government to treat Vietnam with the same dignity they treated Western nations with. They wanted their civil rights recognized, but the government had no interest in doing so. In 1941, Hồ Chí Minh rebranded the Việt Minh as the Indochinese Communist Party.

Hồ Chí Minh wanted to do more than just promote communism in Indochina. He wanted to remove the colonial powers from control, once and for all. He claimed (and not incorrectly) that they were corrupt and power-hungry, and that their moral stance was weak. He used France's immediate folding to Japanese power as a very clear example of this.

Hồ Chí Minh sought support from other countries that stood against Japanese corruption. The Việt Minh reached out for support from China and the United States, both of whom opposed Japan in World War Two.

At this time, the United States was clearly operating

under an assumption that a communist government was better than a Nazi government, which was why they were also allied with the Soviet Union during World War Two. However, after World War Two ended, the United States started to get worried about the support that they had given to the Việt Minh.

Independent Vietnam

In 1945, the Việt Minh and Hồ Chí Minh declared Vietnam an independent democracy—the Democratic Republic of Vietnam. The French government, weakened by German control at home and Japanese control in Asia, could not control what Japan did with the territory.

As part of the Japanese surrender at the end of World War Two, they handed over some control to the Việt Minh and technically gave them control over the territory. However, very soon after this, the Chinese Nationalist Army entered the Vietnamese territory and took over interactions with the remains of the Japanese army. This severely limited the actual power of the Democratic Republic of Vietnam, making it exist more in theory than in practice.

The Vietnamese negotiated that they would continue to be a property of the French Union (France's new version of a colonial project), as long as they were allowed to have an independent government within the Union. However, in less than a year, Vietnam realized that it wasn't going to have success in negotiating with France. France clearly had no interest in letting Vietnam be an independent country. Therefore, the only option that Hồ Chí Minh could see was to declare war on France.

The First Indochina War

The First Indochina War, known in Vietnam as "the French War," was a nine-and-a-half-year war between the Democratic Republic of Vietnam and the French forces over whether Vietnam could be an independent nation or not.

On one side of the war, Hồ Chí Minh and the Việt Minh fought for Vietnam to be an independent country not under French control. On the other side, France and its colonial properties (like Morocco and Algeria) fought to keep Vietnam as part of the French Union. They were also supported by a group called the State of Vietnam.

The State of Vietnam was a government allied with (and controlled by) the French, which claimed to be the rightful leaders of Vietnam. Its chief of state was Emperor Bảo Đại, who had been the emperor of Vietnam while it was under Japanese occupation and abdicated when Japan had surrendered. Now he came back, claiming to be the rightful leader and working with the French forces.

Most of the First Indochina War took place in northern Vietnam, which was a rocky, undeveloped, difficult terrain, making traditional warfare very difficult. Eventually, as the United States and the Soviet Union started supplying weaponry to both sides of the war, it became more of a "normal" war, fought with tanks, planes, and enormous guns. But before that, the First Indochina War was fought with a type of tactics known as *guerrilla warfare*.

Guerrilla Warfare

The term "guerrilla warfare" was coined in the 1700s, based on the Spanish word *guerrilla*, meaning "little war." Guerrilla wars and their fighters (called "guerrillas") are alternatives to traditional warfare, which generally involves powerful technology, large numbers, and (traditionally) wide open spaces where people can attack each other openly. On the other hand, guerrilla warfare relies on small groups of people who are able to move quickly and easily, especially through difficult terrain. This gives guerrillas an advantage when they are dealing with larger, unwieldy armies in unfamiliar territory.

Guerrilla units usually seek out small groups of enemy soldiers rather than attacking a full-sized troop. Sometimes, they disguise themselves as civilians to gain enemy trust. More often, they hide in their home territory, which they know well but is unfamiliar to the enemy, so that they can stage ambush attacks. Moving in small groups rather than huge armies makes finding cover much easier for guerrillas than for traditional soldiers.

Traditionally, guerrilla warfare has been a favorite tactic of revolutionary groups. When a government oppresses opposing viewpoints, and makes it impossible to have a "fair fight" (via democratic politics), and also makes it impossible for their opponents to gather supplies and weapons or forces for a traditional war, guerrilla warfare is the tactic that these "underdog armies" frequently turn to in order to overthrow the regimes that they feel are oppressing them.

The Communists Take a Side

In 1950, after several years of mostly guerrilla fighting where the Việt Minh were almost constantly overwhelmed by the French forces, the two biggest communist powers of the time (the Soviet Union and the People's Republic of China) decided that they wanted to play a part in bringing the Việt Minh into power. After all, although the Việt Minh had somewhat put aside their communist principles in order to focus mainly on nationalist and independence-related goals, they were still a powerful communist party.

Communist countries like China and the Soviet

Union watched the development with interest. It was not yet clear to them how things were going to develop. Would Vietnam be able to establish a communist government the way they had? Or, would its communist party be a brief blip before they came under the influence of the United States, the new big imperial power?

In January of 1950, both China and the Soviet Union officially recognized the Democratic Republic of Vietnam as Vietnam's legitimate government and indicated that they did not want to be involved with the State of Vietnam (backed by the French). They were clearly taking a stance that they were going to support the Việt Minh, and since both countries had significant military power that could make a real difference in the war, people took note.

The Capitalists Take a Side

Just one month after China and the Soviet Union expressed their support of the Democratic Republic of Vietnam, the United States and Great Britain came out in support of the State of Vietnam. They argued that since it was led by the former Emperor Bảo Đại, it had more of a legitimate claim to rulership. They also pointed out that the Việt Minh had been known to use terrorist tactics and was likely to put a very harsh, dictatorial regime into place if they came into power.

However, within a few months, a new concern was added to the United States' fears about the situation in Vietnam. There was more to their concern than a belief in Bảo Đại's divine right to rulership or their concern about the Vietnamese people should a dictatorial regime come into place.

In June of 1950, the Korean War broke out, with communist North Korea invading capitalist South Korea. Both the Northern and Southern governments of Korea claimed to be the legitimate ones, very much like what was happening in Vietnam. China and the Soviet Union were heavily backing North Korea, which was also the obvious aggressor in the war. This worried the United States particularly, as they feared that it was a sign that the Soviet Union planned to expand their influence in East Asia.

In order to prevent the Soviet Union from expanding their power, as the United States was convinced they planned to, the United States felt that they had no choice but to support the State of Vietnam and oppose the Soviet Union.

To Unify or Not to Unify

Both communist and capitalist Vietnamese leaders were in favor of unifying Vietnam in opposition to colonial rule. There was a strong sense of ethnic pride in Vietnam, as they felt that their race had been subjugated by France for so long. Everyone liked the idea of "Vietnam for the Vietnamese," a country made up of a common people being brought together. Unification seemed like the perfect way to correct the state of their country after French rule.

However, neither side could decide the best way to go about it. The democratic State of Vietnam, which was being run by Emperor Bảo Đại, and Prime Minister Ngô Đình Diệm, were also still controlled to a fairly large extent by French influence, and they were not able to make the decision about unification or non-unification themselves. The Việt Minh proposed terms for unification, and the State of Vietnam had no leg on which to stand in order to negotiate those terms.

The French made the decision for them when they accepted the Việt Minh proposal of unification. Unification in Vietnam would be carried out, the proposal agreed, through democratic elections and under supervision from outside countries. Everyone seemed fairly happy about that plan.

Who Should Lead Vietnam?

Letting Vietnam elect leaders under the supervision of other stable countries might sound like a pretty good compromise. However, it posed a major problem: The United States was one of the countries that were supposed to "supervise" the elections, and the United States was starting to get *very* worried about the Việt Minh

They had supported the Việt Minh during World War Two, when they were fighting against the Japanese. The Việt Minh might have assumed that they were going to continue to get similar levels of support, especially since they had been carefully focusing on their nationalist, pro-Vietnamese message. The Việt Minh were hugely successful in Vietnam, with enormous popular support for their nationalist and communist ideals.

This did not sit well with the States. They didn't want a communist party to come to power, even through legitimate means. Dwight D. Eisenhower, President of the United States, wrote in his *Mandate for Change*:

> I have never talked or corresponded with a person knowledgeable in Indochinese affairs who did not agree that had elections been held as of the time of the fighting, possibly eighty percent of the population would have voted for the Communist Ho Chi Min as their leader rather than Chief of State Bảo Đại.

It became clear almost immediately that no party in Vietnam intended to hold a fair election, and that the United States, for their part, planned to use all their power to swing the election towards the candidate that they thought would be the better fit.

North Vietnam, South Vietnam

The two groups claiming to have legitimate ownership of Vietnam (the communist Democratic Republic of Vietnam and the capitalist State of Vietnam) divided the country into two halves, along the 17th parallel. The Democratic Republic of Vietnam took control of the north, while the State of Vietnam took control of the south.

A message then went out through the country: get onto the side of the border that you agree with. People had 300 days after the division in order to move into the part of the country they preferred. People who wanted to live their lives in a communist Vietnam headed north, while people who wanted a Vietnam that looked more like the United States or western Europe went to the south.

Religious (especially Catholic) northerners who feared persecution fled to the south. Communist governments were notorious for persecuting people along religious lines. After all, in *The Communist Manifesto*, Karl Marx himself had insulted religion by calling it "the opiate of the masses." Being a religious minority in a communist country was one of the most dangerous things you could do.

On the other hand, people who believed in the communist agenda headed north, hoping to find support there. Many of them left behind their families in the south. They didn't plan to live in the north forever. Instead, they were planning on staying there for only a few years—to vote and demonstrate in favor of their political views—and then head home.

Unfortunately for them, this was not to be. Once Vietnam was cleaved neatly in two, into a communist North and a capitalist South, the stage was set for a true civil war to finally break out between them.

RANDOM FACTS

1. In 1947, Harry S. Truman said that "the seeds of totalitarian regimes are nurtured by misery and want" in support of sending financial aid to the countries that were decimated by World War Two. Unfortunately, this philosophy did not extend to countries that had already fallen to totalitarian regimes, and it certainly didn't do anything to help the downtrodden Vietnamese before and during the war.

2. The first man to be launched into space was Yuri Gagarin, who was awarded the prestigious "Hero of the Soviet Union" title for his role in the Space Race.

3. One problem that the United States and the USSR faced in the Space Race was that they found that pens didn't work in zero-gravity conditions, meaning that they couldn't take down any notes in space. The United States dedicated a crack team of scientists to create an artificially pressurized pen that would work without gravitational help. The Soviet Union, which was working on a tighter budget, used pencils instead.

4. There have been many conspiracy theories since 1969, claiming that the United States did not

really land on the moon, but instead faked the landing to demoralize the Soviets.

5. During the Cold War period, and especially as the situation in Vietnam became more serious, and the reality of war became both closer and harsher, Americans became extremely anxious about spying and treachery from within. This was a great period for spy movies, but as Vietnam came to the forefront of the imagination, the public's appetite for images of slick, high-class spies waned a bit.

6. In the 1950s, the famous US senator Joseph McCarthy tapped into that anxiety about treachery by starting a regime to root out communist sympathizers in the United States. He said "the reason why we find ourselves in a position of impotency is not because the enemy has sent men to invade our shores, but rather because of the traitorous actions of those who have had all the benefits that the wealthiest nation on earth has to offer." His technique for "finding" sympathizers involved accusing broadly and making it impossible for the accused to defend themselves. It is called *McCarthyism*.

7. Dr. Seuss, author of *The Cat in the Hat* and *How the Grinch Stole Christmas*, wrote a parable about the Nuclear Arms Race called *The Butter Battle Book*. In *The Butter Battle Book*, two groups

develop increasingly deadly technology in their battle over the correct way to butter bread, until they are in a state of mutually-assured destruction (MAD).

8. Hồ Chí Minh became known in Vietnam as "the Vietnamese George Washington" for his resistance against corrupt colonial powers in Vietnam.

9. Today, the Communist Party of Vietnam claims that Hồ Chí Minh never got married or had any romantic relationships, saying he was a "celibate married only to the cause of revolution." Any publication suggesting that he had any sexual relationships with women are banned in Vietnam.

10. In 1945, when he abdicated as emperor, Bảo Đại said "I would prefer to be a citizen of an independent country rather than emperor of an enslaved one." Unfortunately, France didn't end up taking his preferences into account.

11. The United States was extremely concerned about how communism might spread if Vietnam became communist. Future president John F. Kennedy claimed that "Burma, Thailand, India, Japan, the Philippines, and obviously Laos and Cambodia are among those whose security would be threatened if the Red Tide of Communism overflowed into Vietnam."

12. This fear that if one country put in a communist government all the others around it would do so too, was called the *domino theory*.

13. As it turned out, none of the countries adjacent to Vietnam (who weren't already communist) ended up "falling" to communism, but a lot of them fell into states of war or got caught in the crossfire during the Vietnam war.

14. In 1957, a photograph was taken of Hồ Chí Minh grinning and posing with East German sailors. East Germany was under communist control and therefore supported North Vietnam.

15. As the war began, many countries outside the region quickly aligned themselves with the side of the war that reflected their political beliefs. Aside from the Soviet Union, China, North Korea, and Cuba all supported North Vietnam. Aside from the United States, South Vietnam had support from South Korea, Thailand, Australia, the Philippines, New Zealand, and Taiwan.

16. Today, in Vietnam, the Vietnam War is called *Kháng chiến chống Mỹ*—"the Resistance War against America."

17. People in the United States who supported American intervention in Vietnam were known as *hawks*. Those who supported no intervention were known as *doves*.

18. The conflict was extremely controversial in the west, as many people in North America didn't like the fact that the United States were fighting against a democratically elected leader (which Hồ Chí Minh was). That didn't seem to align very well with American ideals of democracy and made a lot of people suspicious of the war.

19. There was also resistance from politicians. In 1964, Lyndon B. Johnson said, "We are not going to send American boys nine or ten thousand miles away from home to do what Asian boys ought to be doing for themselves." This resistance never fully went away, even though Johnson ended up being one of its biggest proponents.

20. The Vietnam War was a deadly conflict that went extremely badly for everyone involved. However, take heart. it ended better (in at least one way) than the Korean War... which, technically, is *still going on*.

Test Yourself – Questions and Answers

1. What was the Cold War?

   a. It was an extended period of tension and rivalry between two countries, but in which those two countries never actually fought each other.
   b. It was a war using thermonuclear weapons that disrupted the ecosystem and caused temperature drops.
   c. It was a war that took place around the Arctic circle.

2. Who was the first person in space?

   a. Neil Armstrong
   b. Yuri Gagarin
   c. Theodor Seuss Geisel

3. What is guerrilla warfare?

   a. Warfare where large animals are used as cannon fodder.
   b. Warfare in which small, mobile militia groups use the environment to get an advantage over traditional armies.
   c. Warfare in which two large armies meet in an open space to fight hand-to-hand.

4. Which of the following is not a name for the Vietnam War?

a. The Second Indochina War
b. The Resistance War Against America
c. The French-Korean War

5. How was Vietnam divided?

a. It was divided on the 17th parallel, between the north (communist) and the south (capitalist)
b. It was divided along the 180th meridian, between east (communist) and the west (capitalist)
c. It was divided on the 17th parallel, between the north (capitalist) and the south (communist)

Answers

1. a
2. b
3. b
4. c
5. a

CHAPTER TWO

THE UNITED STATES IN VIETNAM

There was a lot of tension going on between the United States and any country that *looked* like it might be at all interested in communism as a political practice. It didn't come as a surprise that the United States wasn't happy about Vietnam's new communist government, especially the fact that it had taken on more or less absolute power in North Vietnam. But, even though the States were concerned about the spread of communism, that didn't mean that the US went to war with every single country that took on a communist government… at least, not as devastating of a war as the one that happened in Vietnam. Why was that? What made Vietnam so special? Why did the US get involved in Vietnam in the first place, and what exactly was their plan once they got there? Read on to find out!

1961

In 1961, the United States had faced a series of failures in the face of communist expansion. Over and over again, they launched unsuccessful missions against the communists. Considering that the States had enjoyed a lot of prestige for its military power during World War One and World War Two, this string of defeats was nothing short of humiliating.

They had failed to invade communist Cuba in the famous Bay of Pigs invasion, which had been a national embarrassment and seriously damaged American morale. In Germany, the Soviet Union had constructed a wall between East and West Germany, cutting off movement between Soviet-controlled East Germany and States-controlled West Germany. And most concerning at all for the situation in Vietnam, the government of Laos, which had been a United States ally, had made a deal with their communist movement, the Pathet Lao. The Pathet Lao had expressed open support for communist North Vietnam and had supported the Việt Minh in their fights against colonial French authorities.

The United States feared that if they didn't somehow make a decisive strike against communism, they would lose all credibility. They were already worried that none of their potential enemies saw them as a serious threat. Just as worryingly, their allies were starting to express doubts about the efficacy of their efforts to control the Soviet Union. So, the President of the United States, John F. Kennedy, made a decision: he was *not* going to let communist forces gain control of Vietnam. It didn't matter what he had to do—he would stop them, no matter what.

What the United States Didn't *Plan* to Do

At the outset of the Vietnam war, the United States did make one decision about something they didn't want to do. They didn't want to get involved in fighting the guerrilla war in South Vietnam. Kennedy knew that his troops would be at a serious disadvantage in a guerrilla war, because they were unfamiliar with the terrain, climate, and local culture. He also knew that the war was an extremely divisive issue and that the more involved the US seemed to be on the ground, the more likely they'd be to face condemnation from their allies. It also seemed that getting involved in the guerrilla war would open the doors for a lot more potential war crimes since they'd be in close proximity to so many civilians. Since the prosecution of war criminals from World War Two was still on everyone's mind, the United States were highly conscious of avoiding that possibility.

So, the United States told Ngô Đình Diệm, the leader of South Vietnam, that they would support his rule and offer money, weapons, and aid in developing an army. They would also send soldiers if the fighting developed into a more traditional war. But they didn't want to deploy US troops to fight in the guerrilla war. Diệm would have to deal with that himself. But that didn't stop the United States from slowly (but steadily) increasing military presence in Vietnam. In 1963, there were almost seventeen thousand American military and diplomatic personnel in the country.

The Strategic Hamlet Program, Part 1: Theory

One of the United States' major concerns about the situation in Vietnam was that people in the countryside seemed very likely to be sympathetic to the North Vietnamese cause. After all, they had suffered almost a hundred years of oppression (with varying degrees of severity) under French control, and not all of them were loving the idea of the French simply being replaced by the Americans. There were also many people in rural areas living in grinding poverty who would definitely be interested in the promises of financial security that the communist regime could offer them.

To try to limit the popularity of communism in rural Vietnam, the United States and the South Vietnam government put together a plan to create isolated villages or "hamlets." These hamlets would be artificial homes for people who were living in the countryside. By moving into these hamlets, they would be offered "military protection"—allegedly protection from guerrilla warfare and terrorists, but also protection from the ideas of communism. But it wasn't just meant to improve the quality of life in rural Vietnam. Quite the opposite, in fact. The real reason to move these people into hamlets wasn't so that they wouldn't be targeted by the North Vietnamese military but instead, so that they wouldn't be able to give North Vietnam any support.

The hamlets were financed by the United States and surrounded by fortifications. Each fortification would be patrolled by military personnel, who were given an order to assume that anyone approaching the village who *wasn't* identified would be assumed to be an enemy, and, if necessary, shot on sight.

The Strategic Hamlet Program, Part 2: Practice

The Strategic Hamlet Program would have been considered harsh and controlling at the best of times, and the Vietnam War was not the best of times. Many people agreed that the theory of the Strategic Hamlet program had something to recommend it and that it would offer some degree of economic help to the people of Vietnam, as well as protecting them from fighters who meant them harm. However, it wasn't long before the Strategic Hamlet Program devolved into an unmitigated disaster, with even the original designer of the plan saying that the people executing the program had a "total misunderstanding of what the program should try to do."

For one thing, millions of people were relocated into the hamlets before they had anywhere near the necessary facilities. In September 1962, over four million people were being housed in less than three and a half thousand completed hamlets, or roughly 1,300 people per fortification. To be clear, a *hamlet* is generally defined as having less than a hundred people.

Unsurprisingly, with such intense overpopulation, the troops that were supposed to be protecting the communities were unable to effectively protect them, and in 1963, more than half of the hamlets had been torn out of American military control. Villagers did not want to do anything to upset the North Vietnamese guerrillas in the area because they were not confident that the American military could protect them.

There was also, of course, incredible corruption among the people leading the strategic hamlets. They were supposed to financially compensate any villagers who were displaced by the construction of the hamlets. They didn't. They were supposed to protect civilians. They didn't. Overall, the strategic hamlet program was a complete failure and only turned the opinion of the Vietnamese civilian population against the American forces. In 1964, only three years after it was first initiated, the program came to an end.

The Battle of Ấp Bắc

The Battle of Ấp Bắc was fought between the United States and the communist guerrilla fighters, the Viet Cong. The Viet Cong were also known as the National Liberation Front, and they had an army called the People's Liberation Armed Forces of South Vietnam. Their main purpose was to "liberate" the people of South Vietnam from American "rulership," that is, to spread the message of North Vietnam into the south. They used guerrilla tactics and regular army tactics alike, but were best known for their guerrilla warfare.

In 1963, the United States military detected a Viet Cong presence in a village called Ap Tan Thoi. The Americans had detected radio transmissions from the area and believed there was a small group of Viet Cong militia there, which they (and the South Vietnam army) could take care of relatively easily.

They were not correct about this. They had predicted about 120 people from the Viet Cong, but the numbers turned out the be almost double that. The Viet Cong had also created a series of foxholes that gave them an excellent view of the surrounding area while also protecting them, and they could use the irrigation dikes around the village to communicate easily with each other.

On January 2, 1963, the South Vietnamese soldiers attacked. The Viet Cong had a serious advantage, and both their familiarity with the area and the South Vietnam army's poor training led to enormous casualties in the South Vietnam forces. Only 18 of the 350 Viet Cong soldiers died in battle, while 86 of the 1,500 South Vietnam and American soldiers did. Although the South Vietnam forces had better equipment and *far* better numbers, the Battle of Ấp Bắc was a crushing defeat for them. It seriously damaged morale, as more and more people started to think that perhaps the spirit of the Viet Cong was better than anything South Vietnam had to offer.

John F. Kennedy

John F. Kennedy was elected president of the United States in 1960, and was tasked with the rather unpleasant business of deciding how involved the States should be in affairs in Vietnam. As serious offenses like the Battle of Ấp Bắc just kept happening, it became more and more difficult for him to smooth over the events in Vietnam and pretend like they were going all right.

He hadn't really wanted to be involved in Vietnam in the first place. Fighting had already been happening for years when he became president, but he didn't think that it needed to be the United States' top priority, even if it *did* have to do with the spread of communism, which was what everyone in America was worried about.

Instead, originally, when he was first elected, he had been much more interested in the role that the States could play in preventing the spread of communism in Latin America. That seemed like a much easier and more accessible project. After all, it was right on the US's own continent and thousands of miles away from the communist superpowers. However, it turned out that Latin America was more serious than Kennedy predicted about becoming communist. The situation there became more and more bleak for the American capitalists. Knowing that he couldn't stop communism from spreading in Latin America but determined to do *something* against it, Kennedy turned his attention more towards Asia.

Kennedy, nicknamed "JFK," was a popular president for his young, stylish image. He was the first President of the United States to request that all his speeches be broadcast publicly, which made him into a kind of celebrity. He had a relationship with fashion and film icon Marilyn Monroe, and had multiple other extramarital affairs, mainly with famous beauties. His positive relationships with reporters helped stop these affairs from casting him in a poor light. In fact, he remained an enormously popular celebrity icon throughout his life.

The business of his involvement with Vietnam might have troubled a politician of lesser popularity, but it never seemed to do Kennedy any harm. It might have helped that he died both early and tragically when he was assassinated in 1963, just three years after entering office. People mourned him and remembered him fondly, even though he had made some questionable decisions about the Vietnam War effort. The positive press surrounding him proved to have eclipsed any bad decisions that he made.

The same could not be said of his successor.

Lyndon B. Johnson

When John F. Kennedy was assassinated in 1963, his Vice President, Lyndon B. Johnson, took control of the White House. While JFK was young, stylish, and personable, LBJ was aggressive and domineering. People did not find him as charming or relatable as his predecessor.

Yet, in his early years, he brought in sweeping social reform that benefitted the poor and underprivileged in the United States. Even people who disliked his personality were impressed with his legislation. He supported anti-poverty programs, education reform, and money going to the arts. He developed a policy called the "war on poverty" in which he created jobs and developed better education programs for people living in poverty. Over the course of the war on poverty, thousands of Americans moved up above the poverty line, and rates of young people completing their high school education skyrocketed. People were impressed.

Over the first three years of Johnson's presidency (when he was serving in Kennedy's stead), he was radically popular. His programs reminded people of how the United States had gotten out of the Great Depression a few decades earlier, and people liked it. LBJ won the 1964 election by 61%—the highest percentage of the popular vote since 1820.

However, the nasty business of Vietnam, which Kennedy had successfully avoided by dying, came around to bite Johnson. He took decisive action in Vietnam, sending in more troops and okaying the use of military force to whatever level was necessary. Considering how much effort he'd put into improving people's lives in America, he thought that his popularity would protect him through that decision. But he was wrong. People at home weren't happy about this change. The States were seeing a huge, powerful anti-war movement, which increasingly focused its attention and anger on LBJ.

Johnson was originally from Texas and must have been happy to retire after his time as president to his Texas ranch.

Westmoreland's Plan

As LBJ funneled money into the military, more and more servicemen and women were becoming dissatisfied with their experiences. There was outrage about how the war was being handled, both from a big-picture perspective (should the United States be getting so involved in Vietnamese affairs at all?) and over American tactics (which we will discuss in more detail in the next chapter). Larger than usual numbers of people were either applying to avoid military service or deserting the military when they were forced into it.

With high rates of desertion among the military and a generally increasingly negative outlook on the war at home, General William Westmoreland took charge of making a plan that would win the war quickly and with few more losses. It was a three-part plan that would turn the States' position from defensive to offensive.

The first phase, as Westmoreland outlined, was that the United States needed to levy all its forces towards *not* losing the war by the end of 1965. Morale was down, and everyone had underestimated the strength of the North Vietnamese military powers. The United States, Westmoreland argued, needed to pull out all the stops if it was going to turn things around. There needed to be more men and more money sent to

Vietnam, and fast. It needed to get on an even footing with help from other capitalist countries (especially countries in the immediate vicinity of Vietnam), if that was what was necessary.

Once the United States military had stopped its downward spiral, its next step would be to mount a huge attack on all the guerrilla forces (and the organized North Vietnam forces too). They needed to destroy as many of their troops as possible and take control of the strategic bases that they'd been using to get an advantage over American soldiers. The plan was that this would either wear them down to the point of surrender or force them into defensive, disadvantaged positions.

Finally, for what Westmoreland claimed would be "a period of twelve to eighteen months," the United States forces would systematically destroy enemy bases so that the Viet Cong and other North Vietnam forces would have nowhere to gather and rally their troops again.

Westmoreland was clear that he thought this strategy would guarantee the States a decisive (if probably bloody) victory. It was a very aggressive plan, but everyone agreed, if the United States could put all its energy into the fight, they would really not have a very difficult time beating Vietnam.

But even though the higher-ups decided that this was

the right thing to do for the greater good, they weren't convinced that the public would agree, especially not the parts of the public that might have to go fight in the war.

So, LBJ didn't tell the media any of the details of Westmoreland's plan. He was conscious that this serious and aggressive plan of action with a high cost and an even higher predicted body count was exactly the kind of tactic that would turn people even more decisively against the United States' involvement in Vietnam.

He didn't exactly *lie* about what they were doing, but he sure wasn't upfront about it either. Unfortunately for him, there were journalists in Vietnam reporting on exactly what was going on, and if he thought that he could keep the Westmoreland plan a secret for very long, he was going to be disappointed.

Escalation

When the Americans started putting the Westmoreland plan into place, any suggestion that they should just let the Vietnamese sort out their problems essentially went out the window. The South Vietnam army became less and less involved in the decision-making process, and the United States took charge to a greater degree.

Both the US and the North Vietnam army were determined not to lose, leading to a vicious cycle of escalating attacks. The attacks accomplished virtually nothing except decimating the countryside and harming civilian life. The system for putting military leaders in place in Vietnam involved a quick turnaround time, meaning that most people were not on the ground very long, so leadership was poor. An observer's incisive statement, "We were not in Vietnam for ten years, but for one year, ten times," emphasized the futile cycle of activities in Vietnam.

Johnson tried to keep a balanced perspective and positive attitude in his addresses to the media, but that only led to people becoming suspicious of him. His so-called "policy of minimum candor" (a policy of intentionally hiding the nastiest parts of the war from the public) didn't stop the media from presenting gory images of the war, leading to a loss of Johnson's credibility.

Richard Nixon

After LBJ, came Richard Nixon. He was president from 1969 all the way until 1974, almost to the very last days of the Vietnam War, and his involvement was almost as important as LBJ's. He was the vice president right before the war while Dwight D. Eisenhower was president, and was outspoken on his opinions about the Cold War and the potential threat of communist Russia against the United States. Even before he became president, he was vocally anti-communist.

Although his involvement in the Vietnam War wasn't nearly as infamous as Lyndon B. Johnson's was, Richard Nixon ended up being one of the United States' most hated presidents for an entirely different reason—the infamous 1972 Watergate scandal. The Watergate scandal involved bugging political opponents' offices and other illegal activities carried out by Nixon and his political team. Nixon ended up resigning from being president before he could be impeached (forcibly removed from the office of President).

Keith W. Olson, a historian, blames Nixon's regime for the "fundamental mistrust of government" that has characterized politics in the United States ever since. Despite Nixon's outburst when he said, "Well, I'm not a crook!" in response to allegations of crimes, most of the world *did* see him as a crook, and he has poisoned trust of the American presidency ever since. But people were prepared to stop trusting the government anyway. After all, right before Nixon, there was LBJ—saying that things were going fine in Vietnam while reporters sent back pictures of decimated villages and mutilated civilians.

But back before all of that happened, Nixon was a pretty shrewd player in Cold War politics. He was especially well known for using diplomatic techniques (rather than military) to build better relationships with China and the Soviet Union. With the Cold War under his control, he managed to relax some of the tensions around Mutually Assured Destruction that had marked the last two decades. However, he didn't stop the United States' participation in the Vietnam War. Many people were urging him to pull out, and he simply would not.

Vietnamization

In 1969, Nixon developed the Nixon Doctrine, which stated that "the United States would assist in the defense and developments of allies and friends... [but wouldn't] undertake all the defense of the free nations of the world." In other words, Nixon wasn't feeling great about the fact that the States seemed to be taking a lot of the heat for a war that should *mostly* be Vietnam's problem.

He called for a policy known as "the Vietnamization of the Vietnam War," namely developing the South Vietnamese army and military so that *they* could take care of the fighting in their own country, and the United States would no longer have to deal with it. Many of the relatively pro-war people in America saw this as a very positive approach to dealing with the war. They could give South Vietnam the tools to contain communism without having to send any more American soldiers (called "our boys" by the media) to participate in the actual fighting.

Vietnamization was meant to assist with getting the

American troops out of Vietnam, which most of America supported, but the tactics involved in the Vietnamization plan didn't satisfy many anti-war protesters. People complained that Vietnamization was only going to leave Vietnam in a state of chaos and disrepair, and that it wouldn't fix any of the war crimes that the States was coming to attention for committing.

Operation Menu

The United States continued to worry about the effect of North Vietnam's relative military success on other neighboring countries. North Vietnam hadn't been subdued after years of military intervention, and things were not looking good for the States. They were worried that countries surrounding Vietnam would start getting ideas about adopting communist governments, *especially* if the people from North Vietnam could get into those countries and start convincing people that communism was a good idea. This led to the US's "Menu" campaign in Cambodia.

Since the beginning of the Vietnam War, Cambodia had been struggling to maintain peace with South Vietnam while not alienating North Vietnam (which they were fairly sure was going to eventually win). In 1966, Prince Norodom Sihanouk agreed to let North Vietnam create safe bases in Cambodia, even though Cambodia remained technically a neutral country.

The United States was not having this. They launched a covert mission to bomb the bases in Cambodia in a series of operations known as "Breakfast," "Lunch," "Snack," "Dinner," "Supper," and "Dessert," collectively known as "Operation Menu."

However, despite these fairly successful attacks, North Vietnamese troops continued to operate in Cambodia.

Winning Hearts and Minds

In order to improve public opinion, both in Vietnam and in the States, the American military put together Civil Affairs units, which were supposed to promote popular support for America in Vietnam. Recognizing that even if they could manage a military win, most Vietnamese people would be either suspicious of or hostile to their new American overlords, the military sought to "win hearts and minds" by a series of "nation-building activities."

"Winning hearts and minds" became the keyword for a series of strategies that were supposed to appeal to Vietnamese people on both an emotional and an intellectual basis so that they would be inclined to side with the American/South Vietnam/capitalist program, rather than the North Vietnam/communist program, a major challenge considering the instinctive appeal that communist politics have to anyone living in a state of poverty.

Strategies for "winning hearts and minds" included the Strategic Hamlet Program, projects to improve life for rural Vietnamese civilians, and the "Vietnamization" program that was meant to develop the South Vietnam military and keep civilians safe.

CORDS

CORDS, short for the "Civil Operations and Revolutionary Development Support" organization, was one of the major programs meant to "win hearts and minds" of the Vietnamese people. Its job was to coordinate all the efforts of the States in Vietnam so that the Vietnamese people were getting a consistent, coherent message about what American action in their country was supposed to look like.

Civilians were worried that they were going to be overwhelmed with military efforts, and even sympathetic Vietnamese people were concerned that the States would become an imperial power like France had been. CORDS was supposed to have some measure of control over military activities. Specifically, they were supposed to keep the military focused on pacification (i.e. keeping the Vietnamese people happy, winning their hearts and minds).

CORDS was formed in 1967. Given that the war

lasted eight years after the formation, and the bitter legacy it still carries, it's safe to say that it wasn't a total success.

The Soviet Union's Role

The Soviet Union didn't get nearly as involved in the war on North Vietnam's behalf as the United States did on South Vietnam's behalf. This ended up being a very good idea for them, because their military was able to keep focus and continue to build up strength, while the United States were stretched thin with the demands of the war.

But don't think the Soviet Union was staying out of it. They were very intentionally playing a role that would do as much damage to the US as possible while minimizing negative effects for their own country. They provided North Vietnam with supplies, money, and weapons, helping them build up a more powerful army. This meant that the cost of involvement for the United States got constantly higher, both in terms of dollars and of life. The United States received more and more pressure to pour money into Vietnam, while the Soviet Union sat back and watched their most powerful enemy run itself into the ground.

RANDOM FACTS

1. In 1962, Canadian-born economist John Kenneth Galbraith warned John F. Kennedy against getting too involved in South Vietnam. He said that there was a "danger we shall replace the French as a colonial force in the area and bleed as the French did."

2. North Korea sent 200 troops to support North Vietnam.

3. Richard Nixon practiced something known as "the madman theory." The principle of this theory was to make communist countries like the Soviet Union think that Nixon, leader of the United States, was an irrational, hostile person who could be set off at the drop of a hat. Therefore, if they wanted to preserve their lives, they needed to tread carefully around him to avoid setting him off unexpectedly.

4. Nixon's madman theory was heavily criticized, as theorists believed that signs would be misunderstood and that it would simply cause more aggression.

5. The madman theory has been adopted by Donald Trump in dealings with nuclear nations.

Much of the criticism that Nixon received is being revisited now.

6. The journalist Peter Arnett summarized American tactics in Vietnam when he said, "it was necessary to destroy the village to save it."

7. "Hearts and Minds" was the title of a documentary about the Vietnam War that was released in 1974, before the war was even over.

8. *Hearts and Minds* (the documentary) was most controversial for a scene in which the funeral of a South Vietnamese soldier, including a distraught woman trying to climb into the grave after the coffin, is cut together with General William Westmoreland's infamous speech when he said that, "the Oriental doesn't put the same high price on life as does a Westerner."

9. The first American soldier to die in Vietnam was Lt. Col. A. Peter Dewey, mistaken for a French soldier by the Viet Minh troops while driving to an airport.

10. The United States started a system of air raids meant to stop supplies moving through North Vietnam down the Ho Chi Minh Trail. The air raids were known as Operation Rolling Thunder.

11. Operation Rolling Thunder was only meant to last eight weeks, but ended up going on for more than three years, and involved dropping more

bombs than the States had done through all of World War Two.

12. In 1963, there was a coup in South Vietnam, and President Ngô Đình Diệm was assassinated by his own generals. Considering how nasty his government had been to the Buddhists in Vietnam, and the fact that even the United States didn't want to be involved with him anymore, it didn't come as much of a surprise to anyone.

13. 58,226 Americans were killed or missing in action during the Vietnam War. Another 153,303 were wounded.

14. Casualties for the Vietnamese are less well-recorded because so many of the deaths were civilian deaths. North Vietnam was also unwilling to release their numbers. However, in 1995, they put out a report saying that about three million Vietnamese people were killed during the war, slightly over a million Soldiers and two million civilians.

15. Most of the casualties in South Vietnam were civilian, while most of the ones in North Vietnam were military. Unsurprisingly, the South Vietnam body counts were much higher.

16. At just shy of 20 years, the Vietnam War is the longest war in American history.

17. Technically, the United States Congress never declared war on Vietnam... so, *technically*, it should be called the "Vietnam Conflict." However, considering the scale of the conflict, not many people think that this is a distinction worth making.

18. The Viet Cong used a network of paths through the Vietnam jungle to move supplies and troops from North to South Vietnam. This was called the Ho Chi Minh Trail.

19. By the end of the war, it had cost the United States approximately two hundred billion dollars.

20. No one from the United States was ever officially charged with crimes while in Vietnam.

Test Yourself – Questions and Answers

1. Who was *not* an American president during the Vietnam War?

    a. Richard Nixon
    b. William Westmoreland
    c. Lyndon B. Johnson

2. What was Operation Menu?

    a. It was a series of surprise attacks against North Vietnamese bases in Cambodia
    b. It was a campaign to poison the food supplies used by the Viet Cong
    c. It was an operation to take stock of all the weapons that North Vietnam had at its disposal

3. What was the Strategic Hamlet Program?

    a. It was a program to create fortified villages where Vietnamese civilians would live during the war to keep them away from the Viet Cong
    b. It was a program to put Americans into leadership positions in Vietnamese towns
    c. It was a program to put on performances of Shakespearean classics in war-torn regions

4. What did CORDS stand for?

    a. The Cambodian Operation for Reconnaissance and Disaster Suppression

b. The Christian Operatives Reparation Demonstration Society

c. The Civil Operations and Revolutionary Development Support

5. Why did the United States get involved in Vietnam?

a. They were worried about communist expansionism

b. North Vietnam attacked the United States first

c. All their allies were involved already

Answers

1. b
2. a
3. a
4. c
5. a

CHAPTER THREE

THE WAR ON THE GROUND

Up until now, we've been talking mostly about the big political events that surrounded the Vietnam War. Hopefully, the last two chapters have helped you to understand what sort of events were leading up to the Vietnam War and what it looked like from the perspective of a politician. We've met our leaders, from Hồ Chí Minh to Lyndon B. Johnson. We know what the American military techniques were and how and why North Vietnam wanted to resist them. We've even heard a little bit about techniques like the Strategic Hamlet program, which the United States was interested in using to try to limit the influence that communists in Vietnam could have over the downtrodden peasant class.

So that's what the Vietnam War looked like to a politician. But what did it look like to a soldier? What was the Vietnam War like for the actual, real live people who were being forced to live and die in it? In this chapter, we're going to meet the people who did the real fighting, and learn why the Vietnam War is considered one of the most inhumane in modern history.

The Discovery of Agent Orange

In 1943, a botanist named Arthur Glaston was commissioned to study a new kind of *defoliant*. Defoliants are chemicals that destroy vegetation, so they can be used to clear land when they're sprayed on plants. Glaston had developed some defoliants before, but they hadn't been tested very rigorously. But now, the United States Army wanted Glaston's chemical to use in Japan, to destroy Japanese crops and force them to surrender the war. So, they gave Glaston a huge research grant to study what happened when the defoliants he had discovered were sprayed on crops like rice.

The American army never ended up using Glaston's cocktail of defoliants in Japan (the atom bomb turned out to be more effective), but they kept the chemical around. They also started experimenting with mixing defoliants with herbicides, to create even more effective chemicals for killing plants. The defoliants would destroy plants on the spot, while herbicides would prevent them from growing back.

In the 1950s, Great Britain used defoliants in a war they were fighting with Malaya, one of their old colonies. The war was fairly similar to the Vietnam War (or even more accurately, the Indochina wars with France) in many ways, including the kinds of tactics that the British military was using against the colonial rebels.

They sprayed the defoliants all over the countryside to destroy crops, trying to starve out rebel fighters, and also to destroy the plant cover that guerrilla fighters were using to conceal themselves. It proved to be a fairly effective type of weapon and, in theory, one that didn't involve any actual immediate bloodshed (although you probably already know that Agent Orange didn't get to keep the reputation of being a "peaceful weapon"). All in all, Britain's use of defoliants in Malaya made the United States feel pretty good about the possibility that they could use defoliants in their upcoming ground war.

Besides Agent Orange, there were similar defoliants created, called Agent Blue, Agent Purple, Agent Green, Agent White, and Agent Pink. All of them involved different combinations of substances, different chemicals at different levels, and different defoliant versus herbicide power. Together, the development of these chemicals was called the Rainbow Herbicides. However, Agent Orange ended up being the most dangerous and environmentally impactful of the defoliants, and several different versions of it were made.

Herbicides Over Vietnam

The United States spent about a year debating the possibility of using herbicides and defoliants on Vietnam, from 1961 (when the idea was brought up) to 1962 (when they decided to do it). They called the program "Operation Ranch Hand" and sprayed over twenty million gallons of herbicides and defoliants over the Vietnam region from airplanes.

The main goal of the program was to make it impossible for the Viet Cong and other North Vietnam guerilla programs to use the natural vegetation of Vietnam for cover. They focused on clearing the land around bases and strategic hamlets. They also used the herbicides to destroy crops to try to starve the Viet Cong fighters and get them to surrender, as Britain had done in Malaya. Over the nine years that Operation Ranch Hand was going on, the United States military destroyed five million acres of land in Vietnam.

The people who were doing the spraying were told that the crops they were destroying were going to be used to feed the Viet Cong. However, later, they found out that almost all of the crops were supposed to be feeding the civilian population. With such huge swaths of land being destroyed, citizens of Vietnam were left in states of agony and starvation, confused and outraged at the efforts of their supposed allies and more likely than ever to join rebel groups.

Agent Orange and its Effects

Agent Orange was one of the most popular of the herbicides that were used in Operation Ranch Hand. Some concerns were brought up that Agent Orange might count as a biological weapon, but the United States military argued that it was just a normal herbicide, targeting plants, and had no effect on the *people* of Vietnam (except to take away their plants). A *weapon*, the US argued, had to be targeting *people*, which this clearly didn't.

Well, not so clearly. It turns out that Agent Orange can cause enormous health problems. Agent Orange contains a substance called dioxin, which is extremely toxic. It contaminated everything it touched, including soil (which then transferred the contaminants to any crops later farmed on that land). It also stays inside the human body. Studies today, in 2017, show that dioxin is still present in the blood of Vietnamese people living in areas that were sprayed down with Agent Orange. Even people born in Vietnam after Operation Ranch Hand was over to parents who were affected by it, have large amounts of dioxin in their blood.

Agent Orange and the dioxin that is present in it can cause physical pain and fatigue, cancer, and birth defects.

Peter Lemon

In 1971, a young man named Peter Lemon was awarded the Medal of Honor by President Richard Nixon. Lemon had been born in Ontario, in Canada, but served in the US Army before attending university in the States. In 1970, he was serving in Vietnam as an assistant machine gunner. On April 1st, the Air Cavalry post that he was defending came under attack.

No one had been expecting an attack and the soldiers had spent the last night partying, which might have been why the Viet Cong decided to attack. The soldiers at the base were outnumbered, under-supplied, and under-trained.

This didn't faze Lemon. He took hold of a machine gun and gunned down the attackers, using hand grenades to take care of any stragglers. In short order, Lemon had killed all but one of the attackers, and he took care of the last one in hand-to-hand combat.

There's no denying Lemon's bravery, but there was another factor in his success. During the parties at the base that night, Lemon had smoked a *lot* of marijuana and was still feeling its effects when he went into combat. In an interview a week after he received the Medal of Honor, he casually attributed his success to the drug when he said, "You get really alert when you're stoned because you have to be."

Roy Benavidez: War Hero

If there was one United States Medal of Honor winner more confident than Peter Lemon, it had to be Roy Benavidez. Benavidez stepped on a land mine during combat in 1965, and was sent home to Texas, where doctors said he would never walk again. Not deterred (and against doctor's orders) he snuck out of bed every night, crawled to the wall of the room using his arms and chin, and then lifted himself up against the wall, slowly training himself to become stronger and stronger. It took him a whole year, but doctors were shocked when, even though they thought he couldn't use his legs, he stood up and walked right out of the hospital!

Roy was determined to go back into combat, and he did, where he proved himself even more of a hero. In 1968, he got involved in a battle between twelve Special Forces American soldiers and a thousand North Vietnamese soldiers. With only his medical bag and a knife, he jumped out of his helicopter to help and saved the lives of eight of his soldiers, stabbing the only North Vietnam soldier who dared to get close to him. After the battle, everyone believed he was dead, and the medics started to place him in a body bag, but Benavidez was not to be kept down. He woke up and spit in the face of the doctor trying to zip him up.

Benavidez was awarded the Medal of Honor for his bravery in that battle in 1968, which became known as his "six hours in hell."

Operation Wandering Soul

The American military had some unique tactics to try to strike fear into the hearts of their enemies. They knew that if they were going to win this war, they needed to do more than improving their military tactics—they also needed to frighten and demoralize the enemy troops. That's why they came up with a psychological warfare tactic known as "Operation Wandering Soul."

Operation Wandering Soul took advantage of traditional Vietnamese beliefs about the afterlife. It was believed that, if a body was not buried correctly, its spirit would be trapped on earth and wander aimlessly forever. Burying a body correctly meant putting it in the same burial ground as its ancestors and performing traditional funeral rituals around it. Obviously, this was not a viable option during war most of the time. Because of this, many Vietnamese soldiers were full of anxiety that they were trapping ghosts on the earthly plane and causing cosmic chaos.

The United States military had the idea to exploit this tactic to terrify the Viet Cong soldiers. They created tapes of eerie sounds, the distant roars of tigers, and reverberating funeral music, and broadcast them from helicopters over enemy territory. Some of the tapes also had distorted voices, children crying for their parents, people screaming, and "ghosts" begging their friends to go home and save themselves.

The tapes were, by all accounts, extremely frightening and intended to make the Viet Cong soldiers fear what would happen if they were killed far from home and could not be buried correctly. A Sergeant from the American First Infantry Division said, "Hell, listening to that made *me* want to Chieu Hoi (defect) myself. It must have been effective as hell in the jungle at night."

Ace of Spades

American soldiers had used the "ace of spades" playing card and symbol on their parachutes and helmets during World War Two and popularized it as a military symbol. In the Vietnam War, a rumor spread around that the Vietnamese believed that the ace of spades was unlucky. According to rumor, traditional Vietnamese symbolism held that the spade meant death, bad fortune, and plague.

American soldiers placed ace of spades playing cards on the bodies of Viet Cong soldiers they killed in hand-to-hand combat, believing that this would further frighten and demoralize the Vietnamese troops and make them more willing to defect or surrender. However, there is no evidence that the ace of spades card had any special meaning in Vietnamese culture before the war. It was probably mostly good for the morale of American soldiers. Some soldiers stuck the playing cards on their helmets to show that they were not surrendering and did not support peace efforts.

Liquid Land Mines

One of the most devastating things about the Vietnam War was the effect it had on civilians. Because it was a guerrilla war and involved moving around and relocating a lot of Vietnamese citizens, many people who just wanted to stay out of the war ended up getting killed in the crossfire. One of the biggest dangers for Vietnamese civilians was the web of landmines that crisscrossed their home country. Both North and South Vietnamese troops would scatter landmines, which then had to be either detonated or deactivated. Deactivation was a risky and difficult process, so it wasn't usually done very thoroughly, leaving live mines lying around for innocent people to step on.

An American chemist named Gerald Hurst developed a solution to this problem with his high-powered explosive, Astrolite. He had originally meant for Astrolite to be a kind of jet engine fuel, but it turned out to be too powerful for that. It just kept blowing up the planes that it was put into. However, Hurst realized that it could be put in a can, sprayed onto the ground, and would then detonate at pressure. It couldn't be detected by normal mine detection equipment and it soaked into the ground, so that when it was activated, it would heave up a whole patch of earth with the force.

But the best thing about Astrolite was that, after four days, it would naturally degrade and de-activate, minimizing the risk of innocent people being killed by it long after the fighting in an area was over.

Napalm

One of the weapons that was revolutionized during the Vietnam War was napalm. It had been used during World War Two and in the Korean War, but the Vietnam War was when it really took off as a primary weapon. It's iconic and very much associated with the tactics of the Vietnam War, the way trenches were in World War One or planes were in World War Two.

Napalm is essentially made of a flammable liquid, like gasoline or fuel. But then, that liquid is mixed in with a "gelling agent," something that makes the liquid thick, sticky, and able to attach to whatever it touches. It clings to skin, trees, buildings, tanks—any surface it happens to touch—and it's extremely sensitive to heat and flame.

Napalm had first been invented in the year 1942,

when scientists were trying to find a substitute for rubber. They wanted something that they could make synthetically because their participation in World War Two was causing some problems for them in accessing the rubber trees that they had previously been using, and because war industry was using up a lot more rubber than before too.

They didn't discover the plastic synthetic version of rubber during these experiments, but what they ended up making was no less influential. They developed a powder that wasn't sticky when dry but that turned into a kind of thick, flammable glue when it was mixed with gasoline. The scientists immediately abandoned their plans to make synthetic rubber and turned it into a weapon, adding a chemical called phosphorous that would penetrate into the skin and muscles and make the burning substance go deep into the victim's flesh. Also, when it burns, it lets out a lot of carbon monoxide (as well as carbon dioxide), which could poison or suffocate victims—if the burning didn't get to them first. It was kind of the perfect weapon: if it exploded on you, you didn't stand much of a chance of survival.

During World War Two, immediately after it was discovered, the American military started experimenting with napalm as a weapon of war. They used it in flamethrowers, bombs, and tanks, and fine-tuned the formula so that it could burn at exactly the right rate to do as much damage as possible. And by the time the American military was using it in the Vietnam War, they seemed to have worked out the perfect formula. It was the perfect tactic to use against enemy soldiers... and civilians.

Jeremiah Denton

Getting captured by enemy soldiers has always been a nasty business, but with the advent of mass media in the twentieth century, it became a standard tactic for governments to release footage of their prisoners of war to prove that they were still alive. North Vietnam wanted to tell the public that it treated its prisoners well, to create a contrast with the known war crimes and civilian casualties carried out by the United States. You could say that they were having an image problem that they wanted to correct.

In 1965, North Vietnam shot down a jet carrying a United States senator named Jeremiah Denton. They captured Denton and kept him as a prisoner since he was one of the highest-ranking figures they had been able to get their hands on. Because he was so publicly well-known and visible, they also decided to use him in their propaganda campaign.

The officers of propaganda for North Vietnam filmed a series of videos of Denton presenting prepared speeches about the good conditions and generosity of his captors. It was meant to make people even more sympathetic to North Vietnam, and more critical of the United States.

But Denton wasn't being treated well. He had to get his message across somehow, but he knew he could never say out loud what was happening to him. So, pretending that the bright lights of the television studio were hurting his eyes, he started blinking… and blinked TORTURE in Morse code. The North Vietnamese propagandists who were filming it never noticed the unusual pattern of his blinks, but in the United States, they worked out his message.

Phan Thi Kim Phúc

The mass media that saved Denton's life also recorded many of the atrocities that were befalling the Vietnamese citizens during the Vietnam War. For the first time, war reporters were able to easily photograph the events of a war and get the photos back to the mass media in a matter of days. This led to many photographs capturing raw terror, with no filter between the subjects of the pictures and the audience seeing them in America.

One of the most famous pictures is of children running from a village that the South Vietnamese planes had dropped a napalm bomb on. One girl, Kim Phúc, is at the center of the picture, naked and crying while she runs.

The planes had mistaken the village for a Viet Cong

base, even though it was still full of civilians. Kim Phúc and other villagers were fleeing from the village to try to get to safety at a South Vietnamese base because they knew that the South Vietnamese planes were about to bomb their village.

The napalm exploded all over Kim Phúc and her cousins. Two of them were killed in the blast. Kim Phúc tore off her clothes and kept running, screaming *"Nóng quá, nóng quá"*—*too hot!* A Vietnamese-American photographer named Nick Ut captured the famous picture of her before taking her to the hospital.

Kim Phúc survived the napalm attack, but as an adult, the communist government of Vietnam used her as a propaganda symbol to show the crimes America committed in the war. She was under constant watch until she and her fiancé snuck off a plane on the way to Moscow and were granted political asylum in Canada.

Thích Quảng Đức

Almost as famous as the picture of Kim Phúc running from the napalm attack, is the photograph of Thích Quảng Đức self-immolating in the middle of a road outside the Cambodian embassy in the city of Saigon. Quảng Đức was a Buddhist monk who powerfully protested the war, especially the persecution that the South Vietnamese were carrying out against Buddhists. He feared that the South Vietnamese government was taking a "moral high ground" that they didn't deserve, and that people were buying into it because of their fear of communism.

On the 10th of June in 1963, American war correspondents who were covering the war for the American press were informed that "something important" was going to happen the next morning in Saigon. Most of them ignored the tip, but a few showed up to see what was going on.

Three hundred and fifty Buddhist monks and nuns had formed a procession through the street, carrying banners with slogans that protested the war, the South Vietnamese government, and the leaders of South Vietnam.

At the intersection, Quảng Đức stepped out of a car. He placed a cushion on the road and sat down, cross-legged, on it, while another monk poured five gallons of gasoline over him. He was praying on a set of traditional Buddhist prayer beads. Then he struck a match. Within ten minutes, his body was destroyed.

The photographs captured of Quảng Đức were circulated all over the world almost immediately. People were equal parts appalled and moved by the image of a man looking so calm while he burned to death. It remains one of the most famous images of the Vietnam War—especially of Buddhist resistance to it—and anti-violence.

Charles Liteky

The Americans also had a religious war in their army. Charles "Charlie" Liteky was the American Army chaplain, a Catholic priest who traveled with the military to provide religious services to the soldiers. But Liteky did more than just pray and minister to the American soldiers. In 1967, he and the division he was traveling with came under fire. Liteky used his body as a shield to protect two of his wounded men and carried them to safety in a helicopter zone, even though he was shot in both the neck and the feet. He brought back more of the men to the safe zone and also performed funeral rites for them while the fire continued. For this, Liteky was awarded the Medal of Honor.

After the war, Liteky left the clergy and became a peace activist. The horrors he had seen in Vietnam had made him skeptical of the American military project and left him wondering whether they were really doing the right thing in the Cold War.

The Draft

Every war has gory casualties and nasty tactics, but the Vietnam War seemed even worse than most. However, it's possible that it wouldn't have garnered as much attention as it did if not for the conscription practices (aka "the draft") that the US was carrying out.

Conscription is the technique of requiring civilians to participate in a war whether they like it or not. The United States used it in the American Civil War and both World Wars, but by the Vietnam War, it was becoming extremely controversial. There were too many people who disagreed with the war or who were outraged by the tactics that the US was using. Working class people also felt that they were being unfairly targeted by the draft, because it was possible to defer the draft by going to college, which most working-class people couldn't afford. Overall, the US's decision to use the draft in the Vietnam War was controversial and made people even more skeptical and concerned about the crimes happening on the ground.

The Western Reaction

From the very beginning, people's reactions to the Vietnam War in the States were mixed. Many people were concerned that the war was not in the best interests of the US, that the military was spreading itself too thin, and that they really ought to stay out of Asia's business in this situation. Besides, they had just come off of World War One *and* World War Two, and everyone was reluctant to get into yet *another* war that they thought would be over quickly. However, there was not much in the way of organized resistance… until reports of what was going on at the front started pouring back. People were shocked and outraged at the scale of the destruction. Images like Kim Phúc and Quảng Đức stunned the public. People began to question what was truly happening in Vietnam and why they were supporting a government that could allow such wholesale destruction to be rained down on people who had never done anything except living in a country with a government that the US didn't agree with.

RANDOM FACTS

1. It was actually the president of South Vietnam, Ngô Đình Diệm, who suggested that the United States spray herbicides over Vietnam as a war tactic. He couldn't have known the long-lasting effects of the US defoliant program.

2. Arthur Glaston, the inventor of the defoliants used in Agent Orange, opposed using herbicides in warfare. He was concerned about the effects on both the environment over the long-term, and on the civilians living in the area. He turned out to be right to be concerned.

3. In 2004, a class action lawsuit was launched at the US government on behalf of the people of Vietnam who were affected by Agent Orange spraying. There continues to be a passionate debate over whether or not the spraying of Agent Orange counted as a war crime.

4. The reason that Agent Orange was allowed to be used so widely was that it wasn't *technically* considered a weapon since it was "only" an herbicide. Therefore, using it couldn't be a war crime. After the Vietnam War, the Geneva Convention confirmed that any attacks that are indiscriminately carried out against civilians,

including the destruction of food, water, or materials necessary for survival, is a war crime, no matter what weapon is used.

5. An exact quote is that weapons that cause "superfluous injury or unnecessary suffering [including] environmental modification techniques having widespread, long-term, or serious effects as means of destruction, damage, or injury" are forbidden—a clear reference to herbicides like Agent Orange.

6. The Geneva Convention also prohibits attacks on dams, dikes, nuclear plants, and places of worship, in any way that would threaten the populace. All of these (except the nuclear plants, of which Vietnam had none) were attacked during the Vietnam War.

7. Napalm was developed with the help of big American companies like DuPont and Standard Oil. The project also made use of researchers at Harvard University.

8. The United States only agreed to outlaw incendiary weapons (like napalm) as defined by the United Nations on January 21, 2008, the first full day that President Obama spent in office.

9. Operation Wandering Soul, the American tactic of tricking Vietnamese soldiers into believing they were being haunted, was so effective that

soldiers were forbidden from playing the ghostly sounds within earshot of their South Vietnamese allies.

10. Chemists during the Vietnam War invented superglue. Its original purpose? To put on open wounds to slow the bleeding down until a soldier could be transported to a hospital.

11. Of the war hero Roy Benavidez, Ronald Reagan said, "If the story of his heroism were a movie script, you would not believe it."

12. North Vietnam had a prominent air force. The most successful pilot shot down nine American planes (the US's top pilot shot down six Vietnamese planes), and the North Vietnam Air Force had seventeen "aces" (pilots who had killed five or more people in air-to-air combat) while the US had only three.

13. Phan Thi Kim Phúc, the subject of the famous photograph of a girl running from a napalm attack, established the Kim Foundation to help child victims of war, both medically and psychologically. You can donate to her foundation to support orphanages, ministries, schools, and refugee camps all over the world.

14. Kim Phúc also achieved a perfect score on her Canadian citizenship test and is a Canadian citizen and resident today.

15. The gas used in the Vietnam war leads to an increased chance of leukemia (blood cancer). There are still inflated rates of leukemia in Vietnam today.

16. Eight United States Medal of Honor recipients during the Vietnam War were from countries other than the US, including Peter Lemon (a Canadian).

17. Even when they were being kept in Prisoner of War camps, many American soldiers retained a sense of humor. They nicknamed their camps "Hanoi Hilton, "the Zoo," "Little Vegas," and "Alcatraz."

18. Just because they had silly nicknames, didn't mean that the camps were a joke. Prisoners in "Alcatraz" had to spend all day and all night in windowless cells, three feet wide and nine feet long, mostly chained up.

19. Quảng Đức's heart was not destroyed during his self-immolation. It also didn't burn when his body was re-cremated at his funeral. It was put on display as a relic and a symbol of compassion.

20. The American army won almost every major battle on the ground in Vietnam. However, the massive casualties made almost everyone a "pyrrhic victory"—a victory where the losses were so great that they eclipsed the benefits.

Test Yourself – Questions and Answers

1. Which of these is true about Peter Lemon?

    a. He was a Medal of Honor winner
    b. He was a Canadian
    c. He was high during his most famous battle
    d. All of the above

2. What is napalm made of?

    a. A flammable liquid plus a gelling agent
    b. A powerful explosive plus an alcohol derivative
    c. An herbicide plus a caustic substance

3. Which playing card did American troops believe Vietnamese people thought was unlucky?

    a. The Joker
    b. The Queen of Hearts
    c. The Ace of Spades

4. Who was Thích Quảng Đức?

    a. A monk who committed suicide by self-immolation in protest of the war
    b. A child photographed running away from a napalm attack
    c. A diplomat who tried to secure relations between North and South Vietnam

5. How did Jerimiah Denton secretly communicate with the United States over television?

a. He used American sign language
b. He blinked a message in Morse code
c. He used established American code phrases

Answers

1. d
2. a
3. c
4. a
5. b

CHAPTER FOUR

RESISTANCE ON
THE HOME FRONT

There are many stories to be told about both heroism and tragedy in the Vietnam War. However, in spite of how serious the war itself was, the United States (and most of the western world) has remembered what was happening "at home" far more than what happened "in the war." The Vietnam War was the source of thousands of protests and acts of resistance against the fighting. This was the time when the "rebellious sixties" came into full force, with young Americans standing up against what their government was sending them off to do. Between 1964 and 1973, the "hippie" movement became the most talked about movement of young people that the world had ever seen.

Baby Boomers

Today, in 2017, "baby boomers" is a pretty dismissive term for middle-aged adults, usually standing in contrast to "millennials." Baby boomers are frequently characterized as self-centered, conservative, and belittling of younger people. However, during the Vietnam War period, "baby boomers" had exactly the opposite image.

In the late 1940s, after all the men fighting in World War Two came home to their wives, there was a massive spike in birth rates. This meant a huge number of people around the same age— born in the late 1940s and in their late teens and early twenties as the Vietnam War got into full swing in the '60s.

This is important for two reasons. Firstly, these young people were exactly the right age to be drafted into the army, or to see being drafted in their immediate future. Many of the veterans of World War Two were now too old to fight on the ground, meaning that young people were being sought out.

Secondly, there is truth to the stereotype that teenagers and young adults tend to be rebellious. It is a generalization, but not a falsehood, that people in this age group are often idealistic, stubborn, and skeptical towards anything that an authority figure says to them.

When you combine the imminent threat of being sent

off to fight and possibly die horribly in a controversial war with a natural tendency towards being rebellious and disregarding authority, you have the perfect combination for a huge movement against the war.

Students for a Democratic Society

The Students for a Democratic Society group was one of the first really significant groups that protested the Vietnam war. It was made up of student activists (that is, young people attending colleges and universities who did not approve of governmental actions). It started out as a student version of a socialist organization called the League for Industrial Democracy that focused on education about both social equality and political socialism. However, it soon became its own phenomenon.

The Students for a Democratic Society quickly became extremely concerned about the conflict in Vietnam. In 1965, they held local demonstrations against war all over the country, and that April, they organized a march in Washington.

One of the SDS's major techniques in their war protests was a "teach-in"—a forum meant to discuss and educate people about a complicated political issue. People would gather in university spaces, and multiple scholars, political theorists, and philosophers would present information and perspectives about the war.

The New Left

The SDS was the face of a movement known as the New Left. The New Left was an umbrella term for different political groups and movements that focused on social issues and change. They were interested in improving life for people who were underprivileged and bringing about greater equality.

Today, this might sound like a normal thing for people who identify themselves as politically "left" to care about. However, before the 1950s and 1960s, "left" was almost exclusively about economics. "Leftists" were worried about economic equality and distribution of wealth, and most people who identified as "left" wouldn't bat an eye if you called them communists.

The New Left was different. Many of these people did agree with Marxism and communism, but that wasn't the point. They were worried about social issues. They protested racial segregation and supported women's rights. And they were worried about the common people of Vietnam getting caught up in an unfair and brutal war.

These are the people who we think of now when we think of '60s activists.

The Weather Underground

Even more radical than the likes of the Students for a Democratic Society were the controversial Weather Underground group. People still argue over whether the Weather Underground (also known as the Weathermen) were a protest team or a group of terrorists.

They grew out of the Students for the Democratic Society, but their ideas for protest were a little more powerful. The SDS was known for peaceful protests and teach-ins (with the occasional riot thrown in). The Weather Underground's stated motive was to overthrow the American government.

They opposed racism and the war. They participated in breaking Timothy Leary, a well-known scientific proponent of psychedelic drugs, out of jail. And they planted bombs.

In 1969, they placed their first bomb in Chicago, at the base of a statue commemorating police deaths. In 1970, they bombed a townhouse in Greenwich Village (although no one was harmed). They then started planting explosives in government offices and banks, but they always warned first. Bill Ayers, one of the Weather Underground's founders, stated:

> We were very careful from the moment of the townhouse on to be sure we weren't going to hurt anybody, and we never did hurt anybody.

Whenever we put a bomb in a public space, we had figured out all kinds of ways to put checks and balances on the thing, and also to get people away from it, and we were remarkably successful.

The Weather Underground's Declaration of War

In 1970, the Weather Underground "declared war" on the United States government, in response to police killing two members of the Black Panthers, a black power group that the Weather Underground was heavily associated with. Their first move was to bomb a dance that was being held for military officers at home.

Bernardine Dohrn, one of the leaders of the Weather Underground (and wife of Bill Ayers) said that they were frustrated with the non-responsiveness of the government to peaceful protest. They saw other groups carrying out all sorts of non-violent protests and getting nowhere.

"Tens of thousands have learned that protests and marches don't do it," Dohrn said. "Revolutionary violence is the only way."

From 1970 onward, they bombed (and attempted to bomb) New York City subways and police stations. They even placed a bomb under the women's bathroom in the Pentagon on Hồ Chí Minh's birthday.

Bernardine Dohrn was put on the FBI's Ten Most Wanted list. But other groups across the world leaned towards supporting the Weather Underground (who, true to intention, always issued warnings and minimized damage to human life) over the American government, who more and more were seeing as totalitarian monsters. In that way, the Weather Underground's mission was a success.

Conscientious Objectors

There were many people who objected to the Vietnam War, but only some of them fell into the category known as "conscientious objectors." Conscientious objectors are people who claim freedom of thought, conscience, or religion as a reason that they are unable to participate in traditional warfare, hence the word "conscience." They make the claim that their *conscience* will not allow them to participate in a war.

Conscientious objectors generally come from established pacifist religious groups, such as the Quakers, Amish, or Mennonites.

Being a conscientious objector is always a dangerous game to play. You never know whether your objection will be taken seriously or whether you'll be labeled a traitor and forced into service, or worse. In Nazi Germany, anyone who tried to claim that they were a conscientious objector to the Nazi regime got put in a concentration camp.

During the Vietnam War, conscientious objectors were often required to participate in non-combat service, such as nursing or driving ambulances. Alternative service programs like the Mennonite Central Committee sought to find work for these conscientious objectors that would contribute to the war effort while not offending their religious sensibilities, that is, work that would promote life instead of death.

But not everyone was able to put themselves under the conscientious objector label. Others who objected to the war needed to find a more extreme solution to the problem of being forced to serve.

Draft Dodgers: Why?

Less deadly, but hardly less controversial, than the Weather Underground or other associations along those lines were the famous draft dodgers. Unlike religious conscientious objectors, these were not people who pledged against violence or military service in general but people who specifically objected to the Vietnam War. This was dangerous in and of itself. Not being supportive enough of the US government could get you labeled as a communist sympathizer, and not wanting to go to war definitely counted as "not being supportive."

Hence, the men who decided to avoid the war altogether. Draft dodgers were (mostly young) men who were drafted into the Vietnam War, and, in order to avoid going into the conflict, either intentionally fabricated a reason why they couldn't go or simply "disappeared," either into the anonymous underbellies of big cities or into the draft-free lands of Canada in the north.

Veterans of World War Two were generally outraged by the way that draft dodging became a trend. After all, everyone had supported the war *they* were in! Many older people couldn't understand why the youth didn't feel the same unwavering hatred towards North Vietnam that they had felt in their day towards Germany or Japan. This conflict between the generations tore hundreds of families apart, in spirit as well as in body.

Draft Dodgers: How?

Trying to avoid the draft was illegal, but that didn't stop people. There were many medical reasons why someone couldn't be drafted (including poor eyesight, bug allergies, drug addiction, and homosexuality), and lists of people to whom those medical labels applied soared. College students could also apply to not go to war, and students of religious studies were not drafted by default. The 1960s saw a sharp spike in people attending college, especially in religious studies.

Around 30,000 Americans made the decision to

emigrate to Canada (either legally or illegally) to avoid the draft. Canada, in which draft dodging was not a crime, welcomed them and granted amnesty to anyone who was avoiding the war.

Canada was happy to let Americans in, but America wasn't always happy to see them go. This led to a lot of techniques to get safely across the border by pretending to be a Canadian citizen. For example, at that time, Harris Tweed suits were not available in the United States but were in Canada, so anyone wearing Harris Tweed *had* to be a Canadian. Border guards used tricks like this to smuggle Americans safely across the border into Canada

The Responsibility of Intellectuals

The famous American academic Noam Chomsky wrote an essay in which he condemned Americans who didn't like the war but didn't dare stand up against it. Remember, this was just a few years after the Nuremberg Trials revealed that most Nazis committed war crimes because they were "just following orders," and Chomsky saw a parallel between the Nazis who "followed orders" to kill and torture Eastern European civilians and the Americans who "followed orders" to kill and torture Vietnamese civilians.

In 1967, Chomsky wrote an essay called "The Responsibility of Intellectuals" in which he explains this point. He wrote:

> Macdonald quotes an interview with a death-camp paymaster who burst into tears when told that the Russians would hang him. "Why should they? What have I done?" he asked. Only those who are willing to resist authority themselves when it conflicts too intolerably with their personal moral code, only they have the right to condemn the death-camp paymaster. The question "What have I done?" is one that we may well ask ourselves, as we read each day of fresh atrocities in Vietnam."

Vietnam Veterans Against the War

Students and youth afraid of being sent away weren't the only ones who protested the Vietnam War. In 1967, Vietnam Veterans Against the War (aka VVAW) was formed by a group of people who had actually participated in the fighting. Their mission was to oppose American participation in the Vietnam War on account of the enormous losses and involved. It was founded by Jan Barry Crumb, who had worked as a radio specialist in the war, and who felt that his up-close-and-personal experience with the war was that it was just as unjustified as anyone at home might suspect.

The VVAW supported protection for people who protested the war (including the draft dodgers). They also wanted better health care (mental and physical) and other services for people who had participated. And they spoke out against the use of chemical weapons like Agent Orange and tried to provide services for people who were harmed by them.

Many veterans didn't agree with the VVAW. They thought that the VVAW were being unpatriotic or cowardly. But objecting veterans stood strong against this criticism and spoke out for what they truly believed was right for their country and the world at large.

The Winter Soldier Investigation

In 1971, the VVAW held an investigation known as the Winter Soldier Investigation. The purpose was to expose the way that the Vietnam War was actually being fought and bring light to the war crimes that the United States was carrying out against Vietnamese citizens. Many of the atrocities were the ones that we learned about last chapter, but those were far from the only ones.

The VVAW gathered together more than a hundred people who had experienced or witnessed war crimes over the last eight years of the war. These people included discharged soldiers and pilots, but also doctors and medical personnel, and academics and people who studied the war from a political science perspective. They gathered in Detroit,

Michigan, for a three-day series of testimonies about what was really happening in Vietnam.

The testimony included descriptions of how people were treated as prisoners of war and descriptions of the effects of Agent Orange and other chemical agents. They also talked about the smaller-scale crimes that soldiers were committing, like rape and torture, and the desecration of dead bodies—things that are often considered "part of war" but were against international law nonetheless.

A documentary called *Winter Soldier* was released a year later, along with a complete transcript of all the panels, and yes, this is *probably* where Marvel Comics got the title for their Captain America run.

The Beats

Many of the groups that opposed the Vietnam War were organized, fairly efficient, and politically active in the traditional sense. However, this was also a period of a whole new type of protestor: the hippies.

But hippies didn't come out of nowhere. The hippie movement grew out of the 1950s "beat" or "beatnik" movement.

The beats were young people who happily embraced a life of nonconformity. They promoted recreational drug use and sexual experimentation against the rigidly anti-drug and anti-sex attitudes of the '50s.

Most of them were artistically inclined and wrote poetry equally thick with social commentary and bizarre, provocative wordplay. The most famous piece of beat writing is Allen Ginsberg's "Howl," which loudly protests the "spectral nations" and "monstrous bombs" of the Cold War, while also blindsiding his readers with shocking turns of phrase like, "[they] purgatoried their torsos night after night with dreams, with drugs, with waking nightmares, alcohol and cock and endless balls."

The beats were loud, strange, and decidedly countercultural. But in the 1960s, the strange started to look more appealing, and the beats slowly started to transform into a new breed of social outcasts who managed, at the same time, to somehow be the most fascinating and desirable icons in the world.

The Hippies

Hippies were like the beats in many ways—they were young, dissatisfied, and artistic. They didn't like the way that the government and "established" order of the country were running things. They promoted sexual freedom. They used recreational drugs at much higher rates than the rest of the population, and they loved to shock and disturb people who didn't understand them.

The core message of the hippie movement was "peace and love"—a different approach from the radical protests of the Weather Underground or SDS movements, but one that could exist alongside it. Hippies thought that if people could just *see* the people they were fighting against *as people*, they wouldn't want to kill them anymore.

Although their key message was somewhat political, it wasn't nearly *as* political as, say, the Weather Underground. Because of this, being a hippie became something of a fashion statement as well as a political statement. The iconic style of long, loose hair (on both men and women), gender-bending style, and brightly patterned, loose, Indian-inspired clothes became just as important as the messages of peace. Music and art were also absolutely central to hippies and became rallying points around which people could gather.

It may be hard to believe that a quirky movement made up mostly of young people could have been so controversial. But it was. People *hated* and were *terrified* by hippies, claiming that they were destroying the moral fiber of America. This sentiment combined a fear of their politics (too left!), their sexuality (too explicit!), and their drug use (too experimental!) to create an image of the hippie as the destroyer of classic values.

This sentiment has not entirely gone away. There are still many people who use "hippie" to mean a dirty, lazy, amoral, or short-sighted person. But this has been more or less eclipsed by the image of hippies as fun-loving, sometimes silly but ultimately good people (with great musical taste), which pervades today.

Flower Power

One of the most famous photographs taken in the United States during the Vietnam War was taken in 1967, in Washington DC. It was taken by a photographer named Bernie Boston, in the middle of a march that peace protesters were launching against the Pentagon.

The protesters were the National Mobilization Committee to End the War in Vietnam, and when they reached the Pentagon, they were met with a squad of policemen armed with rifles. Although peaceful protest is legal in the United States, and these protesters had given no indication that they were planning on doing anything that wasn't peaceful, the soldiers were ready to fire.

Out of the crowd, a young man emerged, holding a bouquet of carnations. In the image that Bernie Boston captured, the young man is delicately placing one of the carnations down the barrel of the gun aimed at his face.

The young man's identity is not known for certain. He may have been a young Californian actor named George Edgerly Harris III, or he might have been Joel

Tornabene, a leader of the Youth International Party.

The idea of "flower power"—using non-violent objects like flowers, toys, and candy as means of protest against violence—was not invented in this picture. Allen Ginsberg (of "Howl" fame) suggested handing flowers to policemen in his essay *How to Make a March/Spectacle* in 1965. But this was the most iconic representation. This image became incredibly famous and was even nominated for a Pulitzer Prize. It was one of the most powerful images of gentle resistance and love in the face of violence.

Another photo, *The Ultimate Confrontation* was taken the same day, of a high-school student holding up a flower in front of her face as policemen aim their bayonets at her.

Self-Immolation

Protests in the United States could get just as gory as the ones over in Vietnam. It wasn't all flowers in guns. In 1965, three people who had heard of the Vietnamese Buddhist self-immolations chose to set themselves on fire in protest of the war.

The first, on March 16th, was an 82-year-old woman named Alice Herz. She was a German-Jewish immigrant whose family had escaped to America in 1942. Her parents were denied citizenship in the United States because they refused to go to war on behalf of the country. Herz got her unwavering commitment to peace from her parents, and she set herself on fire in Detroit, imitating Thích Quảng Đức's self-immolation in Vietnam. She survived ten days after her self-immolation.

The second, on November 2nd, was Norman Morrison, a Quaker and father of three. He stood beneath the office at the Pentagon of Robert McNamara, the Secretary of Defense. There, he poured kerosene over himself and lit himself on fire, dying brutally. He brought his one-year-old daughter Emily with him as a source of comfort in the final moments before he killed himself.

Just a week later, on November 9th, Roger Allen LaPorte followed suit. He was a member of the Catholic Worker Movement who had planned to become a monk. One of his fellows in the Catholic Worker Movement had staged a public protest where he burned his draft card, and a heckler shouted at him and his fellows, "Burn yourselves, not your card!" LaPorte shocked everyone by taking the heckler up on his suggestion and setting himself on fire, sitting cross-legged in front of the United Nations library in New York. LaPorte died two days later and lived long enough to issue a statement to the people at the hospital where he was taken. He told them, "I'm against war, all wars. I did this as a religious action."

RANDOM FACTS

1. The Weathermen named themselves after a line in Bob Dylan's song "Subterranean Homesick Blues", in particular to the line "You Don't Need a Weatherman to Know Which Way the Wind Blows," which was about the emerging discontent among American youth about issues like the Vietnam War.

2. There were not only protests against the Vietnam War in the US, but also in countries like West Germany and France.

3. John Lennon was almost deported from the US because he donated bail money for radical groups.

4. After members of the Weathermen blew up their house in Greenwich Village—the explosion killed three Weathermen—the group decided to not accept loss of life as a valid strategy. They always warned their targets in advance so that they could evacuate.

5. Martin Luther King Jr. avoided opposing the war openly, since he thought it would distract from the civil rights goals.

6. The public was not impressed with Martin

Luther King Jr.'s opposition to the war. He lost the support of prominent figures like President Johnson, Billy Graham, union leaders, and powerful publishers. His approach to non-violence was valued at home, but not when applied to overseas.

7. The House Un-American Activities Committee investigated alleged disloyalty and subversive activities. Apart from accusing people of being communists, they also pursued people who did not agree with the Vietnam War.

8. The House was already losing the approval of the public when Jerry Rubin and Abbie Hoffman appeared to one of their hearings dressed as Santa Claus and a United States Revolutionary War soldier. They openly mocked the Committee.

9. In the beginning, most protestors against the war were anti-establishment. As the protests grew, however, the protestors became more mainstream and even included many Vietnam veterans.

10. Great parts of the public saw the war as an imperialistic move by the US and not as a necessary step to contain communism.

11. The media showed live footage from the front, which might have played a role in strengthening the opposition in the US.

12. Americans supporting the war were called hawks, whereas those opposed to the war were called doves.

13. Draft dodging had always happened, but during the Vietnam War, it became, for the first time, an extremely wide-spread phenomenon. The large numbers resulted in 210,000 men being brought to court for it.

14. Jimmy Hendrix never criticized the war openly, but songs like "Machine Gun" and "Star Spangled Banner" became the hymns for the anti-war movement.

15. John Lennon and Yoko Ono were active protestors. Their song "Give Peace a Chance" became *the* anthem of the anti-war movement.

16. Journalist Walter Cronkite published an influential piece questioning the overall success of the war, which promoted President Johnson to state "If I've lost Cronkite, I've lost Middle America."

17. On March 16th 1965, Alice Herz set herself on fire. The 82-year-old pacifist was the first-known person to do so in protest of the Vietnam War.

18. By 1967, 41% of Americans thought the US made a mistake in sending troops, while 56% thought the US was losing the war or at an impasse.

19. In 1972, four Sisters of Notre Dame de Namur stopped and began praying to protest against the war while on a White House Tour. Kneel-ins became a popular form of protest and led to 158 arrests.

20. In 1968, over 1 million high-school and college students boycotted class to show opposition to the war.

Test Yourself – Questions and Answers

1. Which of these groups was *not* against the Vietnam War?

    a. The Weather Underground
    b. The Students for a Democratic Society
    c. The Hawks

2. What is a Conscientious Objector?

    a. A person who refuses to participate in a war for moral or religious reasons
    b. A person who poses a philosophical argument against a war
    c. A person who critiques political acts from an oppositional perspective before they are carried out

3. When was the Winter Soldier Investigation?

    a. 1963
    b. 1971
    c. 1975

4. Who said, "If I've lost Cronkite, I've lost Middle America"?

    a. Lyndon B. Johnson
    b. Richard Nixon
    c. Jimmy Carter

5. Who came first?

    a. The Weather Underground

b. The Beats
c. The Hippies

Answers

1. c
2. a
3. b
4. a
5. b

CHAPTER FIVE

THE END OF THE WAR

The Vietnam War didn't end in glory for the States the way World War One or World War Two did. It didn't end in a glorious battle or decisive victory. In fact, it didn't end in victory at all. The losses were devastating, and the war petered out in a way that was so all-around awful that "Vietnam" became shorthand for a devastating loss. Find out how the war came to its bitter end and what kind of condition the US, Vietnam, and all the players in the Cold War were left in when it was over.

The Tet Offensive

Most war historians agree that the Tet Offensive, in just 1968, was already the beginning of the end for the United States in Vietnam. It was the largest military campaign of the war, with the Viet Cong and North Vietnamese army (the People's Army of Vietnam) against the South Vietnamese army (the

Army of the Republic of Vietnam), the American forces, and anyone else who had leaned towards that side of the war.

It was a campaign of surprise attacks that targeted South Vietnamese control centers. The name came from the Tết, or Vietnamese New Year holiday, which was the starting date for the attacks. On Tết, January 30th 1968, North Vietnam attacked over a hundred towns and cities, which they easily gained control of. The South Vietnam forces were caught completely off guard and had no idea how to react to such a geographically broad and well-coordinated attack. The United States and South Vietnam beat back the North Vietnamese opponents, but that hardly mattered from the American perspective.

What was important about the Tet Offensive, and why it had such a shattering effect on the United States, was that up until that point, they had been convinced that North Vietnam was essentially a backward, barbaric barely-state. It had been easy for them to avoid taking it seriously. But the Tet Offensive proved that North Vietnam had real military power and some serious skill in order to launch that kind of attack. It left the States shaking, thrown seriously off guard.

From that point onwards, North Vietnam (which had felt the defeat more than the States felt the victory) focused on more rural attacks

The My Lai Massacre

In 1968, the United States also attacked the village of My Lai, in North Vietnam. They had suspected for years that the Viet Cong was using this village as a hideout and base of operations. However, if the Americans managed to kill any Viet Cong officers in their attack, it was eclipsed by the atrocities they carried out against the villagers.

Reports are hazy (not many people were willing to talk), but some say that the Americans assembled five hundred villagers in the middle of town. Very few of these villagers were the young men who constituted a threat from a military perspective—most were women, children, and old men. It didn't matter. If the reports are to be believed, the American troops shot them all. This became known as the My Lai Massacre and was one of the most infamous events of the whole war.

Lieutenant William Calley, who gave the order to shoot, was convicted of murder in 1971. He was sentenced to life in prison, but Richard Nixon had him released after only one day in prison, and he was later re-tried and found innocent of all charges—no matter what the evidence was against him.

The Pentagon Papers

In 1971, a series of reports called the Pentagon Papers (aka *United States – Vietnam Relations, 1945-1967: A Study Prepared by the Department of Defence* leaked publicly by Daniel Ellsberg, who had worked on the study. It was the Wikileaks of the 1970s—ugly facts that many had suspected but no one had confirmed. Ellsberg was even charged with espionage and conspiracy, until the Watergate scandal showed that the charges against him were unlawful.

By this time, there had already been no shortage of controversies about American tactics. People knew about things like Kim Phúc the "napalm girl," and they knew that the war was hitting civilians hard. It didn't come as a big surprise to anyone that things were nasty in Vietnam.

But the Pentagon Papers revealed that things were on a whole different level from what anyone expected. Civilian casualties weren't just collateral damage – people were being targeted. And most importantly, the papers revealed that the States had been carrying out military action against not just North Vietnam, but also the neighboring countries of Cambodia and Laos, secretly.

Resistance at Home

As time went on, anti-war protests in America became more and more prominent. Approval of the war dropped to all-time lows. Lyndon B. Johnson had no chance of getting re-elected as president after that disaster, and in 1968, when Richard Nixon came into office, *everyone* wanted them to end the war.

Opposition to the war pervaded popular culture, with anti-war songs dominating the radio and fashions associated with the hippie movement becoming mainstream and bringing their political baggage with them. Martin Luther King Jr. even made a speech called "Beyond Vietnam" where he called the American government "the greatest purveyor of violence in the world today."

There were dozens of anti-war groups, including the "Committee for a Sane Nuclear Policy" (who were focused on ending the arms race), "the Sisters of Notre Dame de Namur" (who hosted kneel-ins and pray-ins as forms of protest), and "the National Black Draft Counsellors" (formed to educate African-American men on their options for avoiding the draft). Anti-war projects were quickly becoming more common than pro-war ones.

The Role of the Media

I can't emphasize this enough: pictures of the war in Vietnam were absolutely *crucial* to understanding why people in the United States turned so completely against the war. Images of Kim Phúc, Thích Quảng Đức, and Nguyễn Văn Lém (the Viet Cong officer being shot in the head), remain some of the most memorable in the world. Pictures like this turned people against the war and sent public opinion plummeting.

Walter Cronkite, one of the most popular journalists of the time, made scathing comments about American military weakness in Vietnam and urged the government to either change their tactics or get out. It didn't even matter when the American military won a battle. The media was focused on the crimes, deaths, and lies about the war, and had no intention of complimenting the government for their work.

The Paris Peace Accords

In January of 1973, North Vietnam, South Vietnam, the United States, and a provisional government that represented revolutionaries in South Vietnam, all signed a peace treaty, known as the Paris Peace Accords, that was meant to end the Vietnam War. It had been being negotiated for six years already, since 1968, but it wasn't until 1973 that the terms of the treaty were good enough for everyone involved.

There were several key points in the Paris Peace Accords that explained the terms of the end of the war. It started out by writing, "The United States and all other countries respect the independence, sovereignty, unity, and territorial integrity of Vietnam." This first line reminded the States that they shouldn't be trying to impose imperialism on Vietnam, and North Vietnam saw it as a victory. There were then four provisions that laid out how peace should come about in Vietnam.

Firstly, starting at the signing of the treaty, there was a cease-fire. All troops were to hold their locations but not continue to fight.

Then, American troops (and other troops with people who weren't from Vietnam) would withdraw. They would have sixty days to get out of the country. Prisoners of War who were being held by either side were also to be released, and any dead bodies were to be sent home.

Thirdly, representatives of the South (Saigon) and the North (Viet Cong) would start negotiating a set of political decisions that would determine "the political future of South Viet-Nam through genuinely free and democratic general elections under international supervision."

Finally, Vietnam was to be reunified.

Why Didn't the War End?

People breathed a sigh of relief when the Paris Peace Accords were signed, but they needn't have bothered. The United States did start to withdraw their troops, and fighting temporarily stopped, but it wasn't the truce that people expected. The peace was uneasy, with many accusations being thrown around of sabotage and unfair dealings.

Pro-war Americans saw this as a surrender. Anti-war Americans saw it as too little, too late. And beyond all that, the United States military leaving Vietnam didn't even lead to the peace that people expected either. There was sporadic fighting after the signing of the Paris Peace Accords for two whole years, until one decisive campaign put an end to the war altogether.

The Hồ Chí Minh Campaign, Part 1: Preparation

In 1975, a major attack was launched by North Vietnam against the capital of South Vietnam, Saigon, and it turned out to be the last. They had been trying for years to get control of Saigon, a major military and strategic base as well as one that would have a huge emotional impact on their enemies.

Saigon had already been the home of many protests that showed relative support for North Vietnam, like

Thích Quảng Đức's self-immolation. But it had been the base of American operations from the start.

In 1975, North Vietnam launched their so-called Spring Offensive, also known as the Hồ Chí Minh Campaign. They started out by capturing Buôn Ma Thuột, a city in the Vietnamese Central Highlands that occupied an extremely important strategic position. Both civilians and Southern soldiers fled the city. The North Vietnam army was ready to attack Saigon.

The Hồ Chí Minh Campaign, Part 2: Capitulation

South Vietnam knew that they wouldn't be able to stand a chance against a serious attack on Saigon by North Vietnam. The United States had been slowly backing away from the war, as it became less and less popular at home, and more and more expensive to keep fighting, and after the Paris Peace Accords, they were following the terms of the treaty and withdrawing their troops (albeit much more slowly than the treaty had said to). This meant that American aid was limited.

The South Vietnam army also didn't have the focused leadership that the North Vietnam army did, putting it at a disadvantage when the two armies actually came up face-to-face against each other. South Vietnam ordered a strategic retreat.

Buoyed by this success, North Vietnam moved to Saigon, preparing to capture it and end the war on Hồ Chí Minh's birthday. South Vietnam made an effort to defend their city, but by that point, their troops were weakened, and morale was low.

On April 21st, the president of South Vietnam, Nguyễn Văn Thiệu, resigned from his position. He hoped that this would protect his life and that the new leader would be able to form a good working relationship with North Vietnam and negotiate with them. However, less than two weeks later, on April 30th, the new leader Dương Văn Minh capitulated (formally surrendered) to North Vietnam.

Protocol I of the Geneva Conventions

One of the many changes to international law that came out of the whole debacle of the Vietnam War was the creation of Protocol I and Protocol II in the Geneva Conventions. These were added to the Geneva Conventions in 1977, just two years after the end of the Vietnam War.

Protocol I was created to protect the rights of people within a country who are the victims of "colonial domination, alien occupation, or racist regimes." These, according to the Geneva Conventions, would fall under the category of "international conflicts," which were what the Geneva Conventions were created to deal with.

Prior to this, there had been no protective measures in the Geneva Conventions for people who needed to stand up against a controlling government. If these rules had been in place before the Vietnam War, things could have turned out very differently, both in the interactions between Vietnam and France, and in the ones between Vietnam and the United States, who could also have been seen as "alien occupation." This convention is meant to prevent governments from creating colonial policies that unfairly or inhumanely target native citizens of a country that that government has moved into and taken over.

Protocol II of the Geneva Conventions

Protocol II was created to protect people who were involved in non-international armed conflicts. Prior to that, many of the protections offered by the Geneva Convention had focused on conflicts between two or more separate nations but didn't have much to say about internal conflicts within countries.

Because this issue falls, in part, under the control of local governments, this section of the Geneva Conventions is less detailed and has a narrower scope than other sections. However, it still protects victims of civil wars and conflicts, such as the ones between North and South Vietnam, rather than leaving them completely to the government to sort out themselves. It requires that everyone involved must still be treated humanely, and that wounded and sick people must be cared for.

Protocol II was controversial when it was introduced, but it was promoted on the basis that, from the point of view of a victim of war, it doesn't matter whether the aggressors are from your own country or not. The Geneva Conventions maintain that victims need to be protected no matter who their victimizers are.

Unification

Once North Vietnam had captured the city of Saigon and the capitulation had been agreed on, Vietnam became a unified country, just like people had wanted from the beginning. However, from the perspective of anti-communist South Vietnamese people, it was less of a unification than a conquering.

The capital city of Vietnam was changed to Hanoi, the capital of North Vietnam. The name of the country was changed from the Democratic Republic of Vietnam to the Socialist Republic of Vietnam. No mistake could be made about what sort of political goals the North Vietnamese had—they were explicit in their plans to institute communism all across the country. They also adopted the term "Secretary General" for their leader, imitating the Soviet name for the leader of a country. The country was divided with a new set of regional divisions, and South Vietnamese people who had resisted the North

Vietnamese government were sent to live in the desolate mountains where they were forced to perform slave labor for the government.

Re-Education

Anyone in South Vietnam who resisted the changes (or who had demonstrated in the past that they held a serious allegiance to democracy, capitalism, anti-communism, or the United States) was required to undergo a "re-education program." This was like a combination of a brainwashing program and a Soviet-style gulag or Nazi-style concentration camp.

They were subjected to lecturing and indoctrination about communism and why they should agree with it. But they were also required to do the most dangerous work that the country had to offer, especially sweeping for mines in areas where they had been planted during the fighting. The equipment was poor, and there was almost no medical attention offered, so the people involved in this particular activity were as good as dead.

The principle of "re-education through labor" fits very well into the communist idea of work as being central to how people think, so the idea was to make people think the way the government wanted them to by forcing them to do work the government wanted them to.

Between one and three million people were put in these camps, including priests, civil servants, and former government workers. Approximately a hundred and sixty-five thousand of those people died in the camps.

Refugees

An estimated two million people tried to escape from Vietnam, mainly by boat. Of that two million, only about 10%—one hundred thousand—made it all the way to their intended destinations. The trip by boat was long and brutal, with few supplies of food or clean water and terrible sanitation. People starved, succumbed to disease, and died in storms or at the hands of North Vietnamese crews or pirate teams.

The United Nations Refugee Agency set up refugee camps in the countries surrounding Vietnam in order to house the people trying to escape, but few people made it there. Some of these camps were in Hong Kong (which was a property of the British empire and would have allowed them access to other British territories), Indonesia, the Philippines, and Thailand.

The people who did arrive in those camps had a few options. Most of them were brought to developed countries, including the United States, but also Canada, West Germany, France, and Britain. Some of them stayed in the countries they landed in, but those numbers were low. Tens of thousands were sent back to Vietnam, either because they wanted to go back to retrieve family members, or because they didn't qualify as refugees and the UN refused to offer them refugee protections.

In the United States

In the United States, morale was crushed by the defeat in Vietnam. People who had opposed the war all along continued to be outraged at the terrible crimes that had been committed in the name of freedom and democracy. But people who had supported the war were no less horrified. People had disappeared from home to avoid the war, and now they couldn't even say that those people had missed out on glory. They had witnessed the deaths of thousands of young Americans in a war that had no immediate effect on the safety of the American people, and now they hadn't achieved anything. North Vietnam had won anyway. All those lives had been lost for nothing. Communism had *not* been contained. There was outrage, anger, guilt, and fear, all across the country.

The United States has never yet stopped thinking about Vietnam. It remains central to the American identity and their understandings of themselves. It was the worst defeat that the United States had ever suffered in a war. The echoes are still being heard in American culture.

RANDOM FACTS

1. In 1971, an opinion poll on the Vietnam War was held, and 66% of all Americans wanted the United States to leave the war as quickly as possible.

2. The loss of faith in government after Vietnam was so staggering that "Vietnam-like" as a label has been retroactively applied to other historical events that shook a people's faith in the government. For example, the 1899 Boer War has been called "Britain's Vietnam."

3. The failure of America in the Vietnam War has generally been attributed to their reliance on high-tech equipment that became useless against the jungle terrain and guerrilla tactics that were used against them.

4. Popular opinion against the war was fueled by governmental cover-ups, and by the violent suppression of anti-war voices in America.

5. Le Duc Tho was nominated for a Nobel Peace Prize in 1973 for his work on the Vietnam War negotiations. He was the only person to ever refuse a Nobel Peace Prize because he didn't think he had achieved peace.

6. Some historians believe that the true goal of North Vietnam in the Tet Offensive was not actually to gain control of all the cities they attacked but to eliminate Southern leaders so that they could have more power when they *actually* took over.

7. The Northern Vietnam leader General Tran Do (who was actually one of the commanders during the Tet Offensive) said that their main goal "was to spur uprisings throughout the south"—which they didn't achieve—but they were happy with the amount of discontent they sowed in the American military.

8. Ironically, considering that the US's entire reason for going to war was to "contain" communism, the tragedy of the Vietnam War may have made many people more sympathetic to North Vietnam and communism. Some protestors, otherwise politically moderate, adopted the symbols of the Viet Cong in order to protest the war.

9. Right before the Tet Offensive, Robert W. Komer (LBJ's special assistant for pacification in South Vietnam) said "something is in the wind." He could sense a dangerous situation approaching.

10. In his second day in office, American president Jimmy Carter officially pardoned all draft dodgers

who had avoided Vietnam.

11. One sniper in the Vietnam War crawled for three days across a field, killed a general with one shot, and then crawled back. After the war, he was recognized by having a rifle named after him— the Springfield Armory M25 White Feather.

12. After the war, the executioner in the famous photo of a Viet Cong officer being shot in the head… opened a pizza parlor.

13. Drug use was highly frowned upon in the 1960s and 1970s, mostly associated with the hippie subculture. But it turned out that the US military had been giving soldiers cocaine and steroids to keep them fighting through difficult periods— about two and a half million tablets over four years.

14. After the war, it also came to light that American troops had been eating small amounts of explosives and getting high from them.

15. It wasn't until after the war that people realized how many explosives the Americans had dropped. It was equivalent to the amount of one plane-load every eight minutes for nine years, or two million tons.

16. A silver lining, though—many of the fuel tanks that had fallen off those planes got recycled into boats in Vietnam!

17. The American casualties in the Vietnam War were much larger than expected... and 39% of them were from friendly fire.

18. The Vietnam War Memorial was constructed in Washington DC in 1982 to commemorate people who were killed or missing in action during the Vietnam War. It was ranked on a list of "America's Favourite Architecture" by the American Institute of Architects.

19. The memorial is untraditional, black and austere in style. Many people disliked it, and journalist Kent Garber quoted an unnamed opponent calling it "a black gash of shame."

20. The United States had withdrawn from the Vietnam War (not that they ever *really* declared war) by the time South Vietnam fell, so they didn't *technically* lose the war. But don't bother trying to make this argument. The effect on America was devastating, even if they *technically* didn't lose.

Test Yourself – Questions and Answers

1. When did fighting in the Vietnam War end?
   a. With the Paris Peace Accord
   b. With the Hồ Chí Minh Campaign
   c. With the Treaty of Versailles

2. What is Protocol I of the Geneva Conventions?
   a. A protocol to protect people against foreign occupation
   b. A protocol to protect people against civil war
   c. A protocol to protect people against nuclear weapons

3. What is Protocol II of the Geneva Conventions?
   a. A protocol to protect people against foreign occupation
   b. A protocol to protect people against civil war
   c. A protocol to protect people against nuclear weapons

4. Who was Daniel Ellsberg?
   a. An anti-war academic who wrote articles about warfare
   b. The photographer who captured the famous photo of Kim Phúc
   c. The military strategist who released the Pentagon Papers

5. What were re-education camps?

    a. Camps for school children displaced by war
    b. Camps developed for refugees to inform them about immigration options
    c. Camps that combined indoctrination with dangerous labor

Answers

1. b
2. a
3. b
4. c
5. c

CHAPTER SIX

THE LEGACY OF THE VIETNAM WAR

Vietnam holds a special place in the popular mind. It's been represented on film over and over again, and almost always by the United States (compared to, say, World War Two, which is a popular topic in almost every national film industry). It's all over books, games, and other forms of media too.

The anti-war movement also made a mark on culture that hasn't gone away yet. Their art and media were just as important in shaping the second half of the twentieth century as the more, shall we say, war-friendly media.

In this chapter, we're going to look at the things that happened in both the United States and the rest of the world after Vietnam, how people look back on the war, and some of the movies and other media that have come out of it.

The Kent State University Shooting

In May of 1970, four students were killed and nine were injured at a protest rally in Ohio, at Kent State University. The protest had been against the American government drafting a hundred and fifty thousand more troops into the war to fight in Cambodia, but as soon as protesters were shot, the issue became police brutality and government tactics, not the draft.

While there had been protests against police brutality before, and many people had objected to the way that anti-war protests were handled, the fact that four people were actually murdered at a peaceful protest shocked and outraged the public.

Ever since then, people have been far more suspicious of police presence at rallies. This is the source of a lot of modern anxiety about the police and the way that they treat people who object to anything that the government might be doing. Today, with concerns about police brutality (especially racially motivated police brutality) all over the media, the ripples of the Kent State University shooting are still being felt.

The Eighties, Politically

All throughout the Vietnam War, the New Left was gaining steam. Racism and sexism were real, popular talking points. Controversial ones, yes, but at least ones that people were concerned about. People were increasingly willing to criticize the government, because the government seemed to be doing *so much* that was worthy of criticism.

But almost as soon as the war was over, the pendulum began to swing back the other way. The most optimistic people felt that they had been successful, so they could relax and stop worrying about politics now. On the other end of the spectrum, the most cynical believed that the Vietnam War had been so terrible and ended in such total disaster that there was no point in even getting involved anymore.

Either way, the 1980s saw people becoming more and more socially (and economically) conservative again after the wild liberal days of the late '60s and '70s. War fervor never again reached '50s heights, but people got pretty serious about wanting the communists gone again. Gains in sexual freedom were reversed as the AIDS crisis decimated the gay community, which had been at the center of a lot of efforts for freedom and acceptance.

Overall, almost as soon as the Vietnam War was over, people returned to form. Nonconformity and rage against the machine were out; conspicuous capitalism was in.

But the distrust for the government, sown by LBJ's lies

about what was happening in Vietnam and Nixon's Watergate scandal, never quite went away. That remains part of the general American attitude even today.

Make Love, Not War

In Chapter Four, we talked about hippies and how they came out of a combination of the Beat movement and the protests over the war. But they didn't just go away after the Vietnam War was over. Instead, they became a part of mainstream culture.

In the '60s and '70s, hippies might have been objects of mockery, but they were also objects of concern, and were maybe even a little bit scary. But as time went on, and the actual issues they were protesting became less and less relevant, they also started to seem more and more silly.

They had worn their hair long to show that they weren't in the army (where you had to shave it off), but now, long-haired men just looked effeminate. They had worn bright colors and eye-popping patterns to simulate the effect of hallucinogenic drugs… but now, they just looked silly. They had dropped out of school to protest indoctrination and the way that school was taught… but now, they were criticized for being lazy and not caring about the world—exactly the opposite of their original intent.

Veterans Affairs

After the Vietnam War, veterans of the war were not treated particularly well, which has led to a lot of persistent and nasty stereotypes about them.

For one thing, people who attended college could avoid the draft, so the people who got drafted had mostly not attended college, leading to them being undereducated compared to their peers. They had difficulty finding successful work after returning to America, and the general attitude towards them was not sympathetic.

For another, despite the efforts of groups like the Vietnam Veterans Against the War, many people had the impression that all veterans must have wholeheartedly supported the war. Considering how much popular opinion had turned against the war, people thinking that you supported it could be a pretty negative situation. Many people, especially young people, saw Vietnam veterans as a whole group as being jingoistic, overly patriotic people who saw no flaw with the war—no matter what the individual veteran's actual position was.

PTSD and the Vet Centers

Because of the high-stress nature of the Vietnam War, many veterans came home with post-traumatic stress disorder, or PTSD. They experienced flashbacks to the war, panic attacks, and problems with their physical health as a result. This made it even more difficult for many veterans to re-adjust to living civilian life. Their bodies and minds had adapted to being constantly on edge, and it was extremely hard for them to move back to a "normal" way of thinking and seeing the world.

In 1979, a public law was finally created to address this issue. Public Law 96-22 established organizations called Vet Centers, in which veterans of the war could access supports, both social, mental health related, and physical health-related. Most of them were staffed by other veterans who understood the specific problems that people were having adjusting.

The Vet Centers were crucial in helping bring the symptoms of post-traumatic stress disorder to public attention. The people working at these Vet Centers quickly identified certain patterns among the veterans who were confiding in them. They advocated for veterans to receive compensation for their psychological trauma and also developed techniques for helping them come to terms with the traumatic events of the war.

Around the same time, the International Society for Traumatic Stress Studies and the National Organization for Victim Assistance were also formed to help people living with post-traumatic stress disorder in the wake of wars and other similar disasters.

141

Protest Music

The first type of mass media where criticism of the Vietnam War really became popular was music. Even today, music is the form that's most associated with anti-war movements like the beats and hippies.

In the 1960s, a sharp divide appeared between two distinct different types of music. There was the "popular" music that was musically orthodox and upbeat, with lightweight lyrics, mostly about romance and love. This was the music that got a lot of radio play and was in line with the popular music of the last few decades.

Then there was the "alternative" music. Some of this music was experimental, using new technologies like electric guitars and synthesizers, or out-of-fashion instruments like acoustic guitars, but the real difference between it and the "popular" music was the lyrical content.

Alternative bands, especially in offshoots of the rock and roll genre (heavily influenced by African-American musicians) were highly conscious of (and critical of) social issues. Hundreds or even thousands of songs were produced throughout the Vietnam War period that talked about the horrors of war and the evils of the government.

One of the most widely recognized protest songs against the war was "I-Feel-Like-I'm-Fixin'-to-Die

Rag," the opening track on the album *Rag Baby Talking Issue No. 1*, released in 1965 by Country Joe and the Fish.

"I-Feel-Like-I'm-Fixin'-to-Die Rag" blames politicians, the military, and big corporations for the Vietnam War—both for starting it and for the disaster it was quickly becoming. It accused them of not caring about the deaths of the young people they were sending off to die. The chorus blithely sings,

> And it's one, two, three, what are we fighting for,
> Don't ask me, I don't give a damn,
> Next stop is Vietnam,
> And it's five six, seven, open up the pearly gates,
> Well, there ain't no time to wonder why,
> Whoopie! We're all going to die!

And the song ends with the sounds of machine guns and a massive explosion emulating an atomic bomb.

Hair!

Bridging the gap between music and theatre was the 1968 musical *Hair*, or *Hair: The American Tribal Love-Rock Musical* to use its full name. This musical was set in a hippie commune, and it was one of the first mainstream depictions of the 1960s counterculture that portrayed them as fully fleshed-out characters, rather than just slightly amusing stereotypes or figures of derision.

143

The conflict of the musical surrounds whether the main character, Claude, will stay true to his principles and dodge the draft or cave to the pressure that the rest of the world is putting on him and go to Vietnam.

While its Broadway-style representation of the peace movement can easily be considered cheesy or "try-hard" today, it was darling—even scandalous—when it came out in the 1960s. Besides the explicit anti-war message, it had a racially diverse cast (at a time when segregation was still the order of the day), and was full of profanity and references to drug use. Live performances also contained a scene where the actors appeared completely naked on stage that had people walking out of the theatres.

Later, a film version was made, with a plot that focused even more clearly on the anti-war message. Without spoiling the ending to the film, I can tell you that it shows, even better than the original musical, how innocence was cut down by the war, and people with the best of intentions were forced into the gory conflict through no fault of their own.

A Yank in Viet-Nam

The very first feature film about the Vietnam War was produced in 1964, and was actually filmed in South Vietnam (which makes it pretty unusual for a Vietnam War film. Some of the most popular were filmed in Georgia).

A Yank in Vietnam is the story of a US Marine who is shot down over Vietnam and has to cooperate with a female guerrilla fighter and a Vietnamese nationalist in order to get to safety. It was heavily supportive of American involvement in the war and didn't have much bad to say about the war effort. All the extras were actual soldiers, both Vietnamese and American.

While it didn't do badly when it first came out in 1964, as enthusiasm for the war effort waned, this film fell into obscurity. People didn't have much appetite for a film that wholeheartedly supported Americans fighting in Vietnam and that portrayed sanitized relationships between Americans and guerrillas. People sought out grittier portrayals of the war than this film had to offer, and it fell out of public favor. However, if you are truly interested in the first half of the Vietnam War and what public attitude towards the war looked like, this could be one of the most useful pieces of art you could use to understand that!

The Deer Hunter

Released in 1978, just three years after the end of fighting in Vietnam, *The Deer Hunter* has been remembered a lot more fondly than *A Yank in Viet-Nam*. It is the story of working-class Russian-American soldiers in Vietnam. It was controversial when it was released, especially for a disturbing scene when the guards of a prisoner of war camp force people to play Russian roulette. The scenes involved real live rats and mosquitos and actual cages used in Vietnamese Prisoner of War camps. The tensely filmed scene met with criticism because The Viet Cong simply never played Russian roulette with their victims. People (especially those sympathetic to Vietnam) said that this was an unfair portrayal.

However, critics tended to appreciate the Russian roulette scene as a metaphor and "organizing symbol" (as Roger Ebert put it), rather than an actual portrayal of war crimes. Critical reception (and the majority of audience reception) was wildly positive, both on its release and since. *The Deer Hunter* has been praised as one of the greatest films of all times, including being named the "fifty-third greatest American film of all time" in 2007 by the American Film Institute.

What makes *The Deer Hunter* so significant, aside from being a tense and well-crafted piece of art and storytelling, is its portrayal of complex characters within the war and its treatment of Vietnam as a true epic.

Apocalypse Now

Maybe the most iconic film set in the Vietnam War, *Apocalypse Now* combines epic director Francis Ford

Coppola, epic actors Marlon Brando, Martin Sheen, and Robert Duvall, and epic modern novella *Heart of Darkness* to create, well, an epic.

Apocalypse Now was a disaster while it was being filmed. Sets were destroyed by extreme weather, and Martin Sheen had a heart attack on location. However, it later gained renown as one of the greatest films of history. *Sight & Sound* ranked it as the fourteenth best film ever made in 2012, and the Library of Congress selected it for preservation for being unusually "culturally, historically, or aesthetically significant." Roger Ebert called it the greatest film on the Vietnam War. The single line, "I love the smell of napalm in the morning," has reached iconic status that most films can only dream of.

Apocalypse Now portrayed the Vietnam War with grit, scale, and a kind of drama that has never been achieved by any other film in quite the same way. Even if you haven't seen it, scenes and images from it are inescapable in modern American culture. It is probably better-remembered than any actual event from the Vietnam War and colors many people's perception of the events.

Full Metal Jacket

Full Metal Jacket was produced by Stanley Kubrick, director of *The Shining*, and one of the most famous filmmakers of the twentieth century. He was heavily involved with filmmaking all during the Vietnam War and Cold War periods. Some people even claimed that he was responsible for filming a fake moon landing in 1969.

Full Metal Jacket, which was released in 1987, is Kubrick's war epic, the story of a platoon of Marines being trained and deployed into the Tet Offensive. It represents the brutality of the war, showing how men were forced to be unnaturally brutal, and the effect that that can have on the mind.

Its portrayal of boot camp drew a lot of attention, as people saw it as portraying military training as a kind of brainwashing. It's hard to say whether that was Kubrick's intended message or not, but that message certainly wouldn't have been out of place in the Vietnam War period. Many people did indeed see the training that soldiers had to undergo as a kind of brainwashing, as they were forced to pledge themselves one hundred percent—even lay down their lives—for a cause that dwindling numbers actually believed in.

The Punisher

Frank Castle, aka The Punisher is a Marvel Comics character who fought in the Vietnam War. Marvel has never shied away from depictions of war in their comics, and the Punisher is just one example.

He fought during Vietnam and developed techniques for combat that he uses in his life as a superhero vigilante. But his character learned more than just how to kill people during the war. He also developed his acute sense of personal justice and his will to punish the guilty as violently as they need to be punished.

Castle's appearance on screen in the Marvel Netflix series *Daredevil* also alludes to the fact that he is probably suffering from acute post-traumatic stress disorder. Because of this, he has difficulty forming meaningful relationships, and he doesn't feel any sense of guilt when he commits murder, as long as he feels like the person he's killing deserved it. Skewed senses of morality are hallmarks of many (although not all) people's experiences of post-traumatic stress disorder.

Vietnam in Video Games

Vietnam is a hugely popular setting for video and computer games, especially in the hugely lucrative first-person shooter genre. The very first video game set in Vietnam was simply called "Vietnam" and was put out in 1986. Since then, there have been dozens of other games put out that use this war as a setting. These include ones based on films like both the 1985 and 1987 *Rambo* games. There are also games that are part of larger series, like 2010's *Call of Duty: Black Ops*, or the *Battlefield Vietnam* expansion to the *Battlefield 1942* game.

Depictions of Vietnam in video games are controversial. In fact, depictions of any war in video games can be controversial. Many people feel that video games glorify violence in whatever war they are presenting, because they encourage (in fact, require) the player to actually participate in the violence. While many people feel this might be excusable if you're shooting, say, Nazis or completely fictional soldiers, it's a little more questionable to recreate the Vietnam War in game form. For one thing, it was recent, and a huge percentage of the survivors are still alive today. For another, it was such a controversial war at the time, and ideas about who was in the right and the who was in the wrong were so skewed, that pretending to kill people (usually Viet Cong) can seem a bit tasteless.

The gaming industry is certainly not going to stop making Vietnam games anytime soon. The criticism is too weak to make up for how lucrative the games often are! But the controversy is never far from people's minds when a new game about blowing up Viet Cong or dropping napalm bombs hits the shelf, and even seasoned gamers might choose not to participate.

Vietnam in Comedy

Not all movies and books about Vietnam are dark, gritty, and depressing. Some are, perhaps oddly, a little goofy.

For example, in 1987 (less than fifteen years after the end of fighting), the world-famous comic actor Robin Williams starred in *Good Morning, Vietnam* — not an out-and-out comedy but certainly an unusually comedic take on the war for just a few years after it had ended! Williams' character is an irreverent radio DJ whose broadcasts boost the moods of the troops but don't sit well with the upper levels of the military. The story was based loosely on the career of Adrian Cronauer, an Air Force sergeant and actual Vietnam War DJ. It may also have been inspired by stories of soldiers' moods being boosted even by American protest music during the fighting, just because it reminded them that there was still something outside what seemed like a brutal and hopeless situation.

Another famous comedy with a background in the Vietnam War is *Forrest Gump*, an adaptation of a novel by Winston Groom. *Forrest Gump* is the story of the titular Forrest, a slightly disabled man who fought in the Vietnam War. Despite his "marginal intelligence," people find him charming, and he proves himself to be a hero and is even awarded a Medal of Honor for his bravery during conflict. The film *Forrest Gump* isn't primarily about the Vietnam War, but it takes an unusually positive look at it, showing how it built comradery and character in the people who served.

Unlike, say, some World War Two comedies, the tone of both these films was tender and cheerful but still respectful and ultimately somewhat serious. There may be some more time needed before we can expect a zany, out-and-out comedy set in Vietnam to gain any real popular appeal.

Where to From Here?

More than any other war, the Vietnam War has shaped American society today. It's still impossible to say what kind of impact the war is going to have for the next twenty, fifty, or hundred years—the "shock waves" haven't even started to fade.

Vietnam is still being ruled by the communist government that the United States and South Vietnam worked so hard to prevent from gaining power. Quality of life in Vietnam is not as terrible as anticipated, with moderate safety and a good cost of living in many cities. Although it is under a communist government, it's been undergoing a process of economic liberalization, moving more and more towards capitalism and away from a governmentally regulated economy. In the 1980s, it was a country in ruins, and its recovery has been relatively good.

The United States was not decimated in numbers or environmental impact the way that Vietnam was, but it was still shaken deeply by the war. Not since the American Civil War had the American people been so deeply divided on a war, nor had any war changed popular culture in the way that culture changed from the '50s "square" to the '60s hippie. We are going to continue to see Vietnam on film, in books and games, and reflected in our politics.

So, every time Donald Trump uses Nixon's madman technique to intimidate a nuclear nation, or every time someone says that they think the government might be lying about what they're doing in a war, or every time you hear someone talk about baby boomers, you can look back on what you've learned about the Vietnam War.

RANDOM FACTS

1. The highest grossing film about the Vietnam War is not *Apocalypse Now, The Deer Hunter,* or even *Forrest Gump.* It's *Rambo: First Blood Part II,* at $300 million.

2. The success of *Rambo: First Blood Part II,* in spite of it being radically historically inaccurate and portraying one man single-handedly taking out the entire Vietnamese army, does not sit well with historians.

3. In 1967, Martin Scorsese directed a six-minute film called "The Big Shave." The entire film is of a man shaving, but according to Scorsese (and the film's alternate title "Viet '67"), the film is actually about Vietnam.

4. Even though the Vietnam War has been the subject of so many films, it still can't hold a candle to World War Two. The highest grossing World War Two film is *Dunkirk,* with $462 million, and there are many more WWII films in the top ten than Vietnam films.

5. In an article called "The Vietnam Oscars," Peter Biskind attempted to identify what exactly the political message of *The Deer Hunter* was. He

ultimately defended the film as not having a harmful agenda when he said, "It may have been a mere by-product of Hollywood myopia, the demands of the war-film genre, garden-variety American parochialism, and simple ignorance, than it was the pre-meditated right-wing roadmap it seemed to many."

6. The original plan for *Apocalypse Now* was to have it directed by Steven Spielberg and shot in black-and-white as a faux documentary.

7. "I-Feel-Like-I'm-Fixin'-to-Die Rag" was broadcast to prisoners in the Hỏa Lò Prison, a North Vietnam Prisoner of War camp nicknamed the "Hanoi Hilton." The North Vietnam army hoped that it would destroy their morale by showing them how negatively they were being viewed by people at home.

8. While there were undoubtedly some people who were discouraged by listening to "I-Feel-Like-I'm-Fixin'-to-Die Rag" in prison, most of the prisoners said that it boosted their mood and that they enjoyed singing along to it, much to the annoyance of their captors.

9. The protest song "Alice's Restaurant" told a story about the Vietnam War that was later adapted into a film.

10. John Wayne starred in a film about Vietnam

called *The Green Beret*, which was extremely pro-war and can be essentially considered propaganda by modern standards.

11. John Wayne did not serve in the Vietnam War.

12. Walt Disney Pictures made the odd decision to make a film called *Operation Dumbo Drop* set in the Vietnam War. It is another of the slightly comedic but ultimately sincere Vietnam War films, but has not been remembered nearly as fondly as the likes of *Good Morning Vietnam* or *Forrest Gump*, in part because it doesn't have the dark edge that even those two have.

13. It was, however, based on the true story of a Green Beret American soldier named John Scott Gantt who *did* air-lift a pair of elephants across the country.

14. Nguyen Hoa Giai, a former Viet Cong guerrilla, did an interview with Evan V. Symon in 2015 where he presented the little-heard Vietnamese perspective on the war.

15. Nguyen described how the war was brutally difficult for the rebel fighters too, especially when they had to stay in unfamiliar jungle territory. He related the story of how one of his friends was bitten by a huge centipede, and while the centipede wasn't toxic, his friend died anyway—from suicide because the pain was so

intense.

16. Nguyen also had something good to say about the effect of communism on Vietnam. It meant that he had much-needed social interaction after the war. In the United States, systems like the Vet Centers provided that for veterans, but in communist Vietnam, that kind of human contact was just part of the culture.

17. In spite of the difficult time that Vietnam veterans face, and the vocal criticism they received soon after returning from the war, 87% of Americans describe their feelings for Vietnam veterans as "very high esteem."

18. Vets are also less likely to go to jail than the general public! Only 0.5% of Vietnam veterans have served jail time

19. British philosopher Bertrand Russell organized a tribunal to evaluate American conduct in Vietnam, which concluded that the government was guilty of genocide. This did not make an impact.

20. There are 1,611 Americans who are unaccounted for and considered still missing in the Vietnam area.

Test Yourself – Questions and Answers

1. Which film was made most recently?

    a. Full Metal Jacket
    b. A Yank in Viet-Nam
    c. Apocalypse Now

2. Which of these is not a protest song?

    a. I-Feel-Like-I'm-Fixing-to-Die-Rag
    b. Alice's Restaurant
    c. Lucy in the Sky with Diamonds

3. What were Vet Centers?

    a. Centers where Vietnam War veterans could access supports and services
    b. Governmental bureaus for keeping statistics on veterans
    c. Clinics for animals affected by the Vietnam War

4. Which Marvel character fought in the Vietnam War?

    a. Captain America
    b. The Punisher
    c. Thor

5. What challenges did American Vietnam War veterans face on returning to the United States?

    a. Difficulty dealing with mental health issues

stemming from trauma

b. Poor education, compared to some of their peers

c. Assumptions that they supported the war because they fought in it

d. All of the above

Answers

1. a
2. c
3. a
4. b
5. d

DON'T FORGET YOUR
FREE BOOKS

MORE BOOKS BY BILL O'NEILL

I hope you enjoyed this book and learned something new. Please feel free to check out some of my previous books on Amazon.

Made in the USA
Coppell, TX
27 December 2022

90790002R00096